DETAIL IN CONTEMPORARY LIGHTING DESIGN

LAURENCE KING

Published in 2012 by
Laurence King Publishing Ltd
361–373 City Road
London
EC1V 1LR
e-mail: enquiries@laurenceking.com
www.laurenceking.com

A catalogue record for this book is
available from the British Library

ISBN: 978 1 78067 010 2

Designed by The Urban Ant Ltd
Project Editor: Gaynor Sermon
Cover design by Hamish Muir

Printed in China

DETAIL IN CONTEMPORARY LIGHTING DESIGN

JILL ENTWISTLE

LAURENCE KING PUBLISHING

CONTENTS

INTRODUCTION

For a commodity so fundamental to our existence, it has taken us a long time to recognize the importance of light in our built environment. Or rather its importance has been recognized, by everyone from the Romans to Le Corbusier, but it has perhaps not always been afforded the respect and attention it deserves in our workplaces, retail and leisure environments, or our homes. A number of developments over the past five decades, and especially the last 20 years, has significantly changed that.

The emergence of a specialist lighting design profession over this period has done much to promote awareness that lighting is not simply a matter of calculating lux levels or choosing fittings because they are aesthetically pleasing rather than on the basis of the quality of light they produce. Light is both an art and a science. As Norman Foster put it: 'If the spaces that we create do not move the heart and mind then they are surely only addressing one part of their function. Any engineer can quantify light by which to read a book. But what about the poetic dimension of natural light: the changing nature of an overcast sky, the discovery of shade, the luminosity of a patch of sunlight?'

Discussing the 1980s, when lighting design in Europe and especially the UK began its significant development, one leading lighting designer has spoken of 'a real thirst from architects to find an alternative to the engineering-led, predictive and formula-based approach to architectural and environmental lighting. Architects were seeking a sympathetic understanding of their architectural expression from those who knew what was technologically possible and who could also, when required, create an additional dimension to their work. It felt as if a long-awaited expectation and need by architects had finally been answered.'

Light and shadow are crucial to our understanding, our enjoyment and our ability to use a space effectively. But as well as Foster's 'poetic dimension of light' there are other prosaic but important aspects that have driven the importance of lighting design as a separate discipline. Saving lighting energy, for example, requires a particular expertise if efficient electric light sources are to be used without compromising the quality of the lit environment. It also requires skill to exploit natural light to this end: determining building massing, orientation, active and passive control of daylight, and so on.

There is also the matter of technology. The emergence of LEDs from behind the control console and their evolution into a viable general white light source has been one of the most remarkable recent developments in lighting. In conjunction with control systems, which are now becoming a de facto element in any lighting scheme, they have been hailed as a panacea for our energy profligacy, but, as with any new technology, specifying solid state lighting without expert guidance can be a minefield and frequently LEDs are not the optimum option in terms of cost and reliability when compared to conventional efficient sources such as fluorescent and metal halide.

As well as being the fourth dimension of architecture, lighting has a series of functional roles beyond simply rendering our surroundings visible. It reveals the richness of materials – the rough texture of concrete, the translucence of etched glass, the gleam of polished granite. 'Light has not just intensity, but also vibration, which is capable of roughening a smooth material, of giving three-dimensional quality to a flat surface,' said acclaimed Italian architect Renzo Piano. The eye is attracted to areas of brightness so it also plays a navigational role, showing the hierarchy of a space – highlighting the hotel reception, the lift lobby or the merchandise on display. Most obviously it creates atmosphere, playing an almost semiotic role in denoting an upmarket ambience or a discouraging brightness – the delineation between the moody Michelin-starred restaurant and the fluorescent-flooded fast-food outlet.

A further development that has made us examine light more closely is the discovery of a third receptor in the human eye. It seems that light also has a non-visual effect on the body, via the pineal gland to the circadian system. Lighting design is about providing a functional, comfortable and aesthetic context for human beings to work and play in. If light has an effect on our body clock, and therefore our sense of wellbeing, it is important to understand that process and create conducive illumination. Seasonal affective disorder, or SAD, is one of the more extreme examples of the effect that light, or the lack of it, can exert. The body of research in this area suggests that the colour temperature and dynamism of white light could be important to how we feel and how productive we are. Increasingly in the workplace environment we are seeing bio-dynamic lighting systems that shift from cool to warm colour temperatures according to the time of day and the natural daylight pattern outside.

Linked to this is the recognition of our need for visual stimulation. The dappled natural light of a wood or the play of sunshine on water delights us. The disparity between those environments and an office uniformly lit by endless arrays of fluorescent downlighting is only too evident. This acknowledgement of the psychological and physical effects of lighting has led to more illumination on vertical surfaces and ceilings, and certainly in the workplace has led to a welcome transition from the dark and oppressive overhead planes created by the now-dated louvered fitting.

All lighting schemes should, of course, be a carefully balanced composition, a judicious combination of light and shadow, less light and more light, cool light and warm light. Contrast, and an equal emphasis on what is not lit as much as what is lit, are key to creating the overall effect. However, the purpose of this book is to focus on specific details, examining more closely how particular effects are achieved.

Some of the schemes are very simple and are not necessarily concerned with lighting pyrotechnics. Backlighting, for instance, is not a groundbreaking technique, but it is technically exacting if an even illumination is to be achieved, or if the exact characteristics of daylight are to be reproduced to display a glass artwork as it was designed to be shown. In the case of the backlit office mural, it is also an inspirational example of how a lit component can become a cornerstone of an interior.

There is arguably now an overuse of coloured lighting in inappropriate settings, a situation exacerbated by the emergence of LEDs and the crossover of theatrically based DMX control systems into the architectural arena. Too often the inexpert succumb to the temptation to use as many of the 16 million hues on offer as possible through such technology. As always, context is everything. The nightclub and other leisure venues are the traditional candidates for the visual excitement of animation and colour changing. But used judiciously, and with a meaningful palette, coloured lighting can make a powerful statement even in such conservative surroundings as a corporate atrium. Most schemes, however, show that while more subtle, white light schemes are often the most compelling and evocative.

Whether featuring an overt decorative element or a discreet lighting effect, what many schemes included in this book also demonstrate is that the most successful outcomes are generally those where lighting is considered at the earliest possible stage so that it can be integrated into the architecture. As well as creating a seamless result where the light is paramount and the fittings carefully concealed, this also allows consideration of the finishes, which can have an enormous impact on the lit space. The switch from white to black or from gloss to matt will have a profound effect on the resultant light levels (either too much or too little), and create issues such as unwanted reflections and glare, as the surrounding materials accordingly absorb, reflect and refract the light. Lighting and architecture must be viewed as a composite, and the closer the collaboration between architect/interior designer and lighting designer the more harmonious and successful the result.

'Light is the greatest magic of all, for all other magic flows from it,' said Richard Rogers. 'Without light there is no life. Without life there is no creation, no art, no architecture, no vision and no expression. Seize light, celebrate light, design with light, and enjoy light.'

Jill Entwistle

ACKNOWLEDGMENTS

My thanks to all the lighting designers who have contributed material and who endured seemingly endless requests for information and material with extraordinary patience. Jessica Burke of the IALD was very helpful in finding some of the projects. Vanessa Green has done a superb job on the design, and Gaynor Sermon has been an assiduous and very supportive editor, ever calm and good-humoured. Vic Brand also more than deserves a mention for the painstaking task of final-checking drawings and calculating missing scales. Finally, my thanks to my partner Francis Pearce who had to put up with me throughout the whole protracted process.

COMMERCIAL AND PUBLIC

133 HOUNDSDITCH, LONDON
MAURICE BRILL
LIGHTING DESIGN

An important aim of the refurbishment of this 1980s City office was to transform the atrium area where the reception is located from a dark, lacklustre entrance to an airy, welcoming and more easily navigable space. The backbone of the design is a strong black feature wall, which ribbons from the entrance, wrapping behind the reception before ascending up into the atrium. Opposite to this is a rough-textured limestone wall that wraps deep into the lift lobby at the rear of the reception.

The ambition for the lighting was both to create a sense of space beyond space – drawing people in and through to the lift lobby at the back – and to create a simple but strong change from day to night. The focus is on the inclined black stone feature wall (nearly all of the walls are sloping). During the day, 70W ceramic metal halide, ground-recessed uplights accent the wall form and texture (an effect which is echoed in reverse by the up/downlights on the textured limestone wall). At night, the uplights are switched off, allowing the white LED edgelit acrylic blades mounted between the stone panels to come to the fore, creating an abstract pattern that delineates the wall through into the atrium. The result is a shift in emphasis, moving away from form to defining space. All the LED blades were custom made to match the tile widths. Each section had to be cut at different angles in order to create a parallel surface and match the wall's mounting angle.

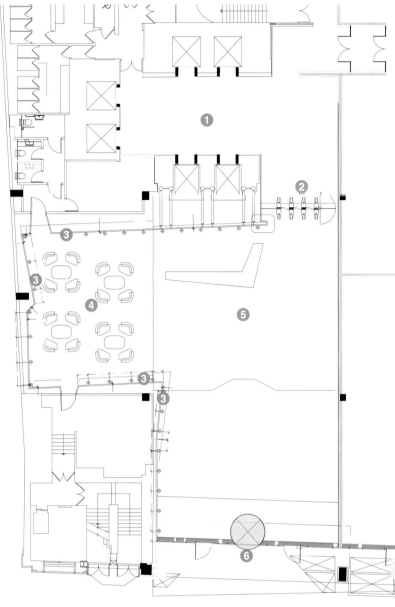

SCALE 1:250

ABOVE RIGHT
Floor plan of reception showing extent
of LED wrap wall
1 Lift lobby
2 Security turnstiles
3 LED wrap wall
4 Client waiting area
5 Reception area and atrium
6 Entrance

OPPOSITE
At night, white edgelit acrylic blades
form an abstract pattern on the wall
that ribbons from the entrance before
ascending behind the reception

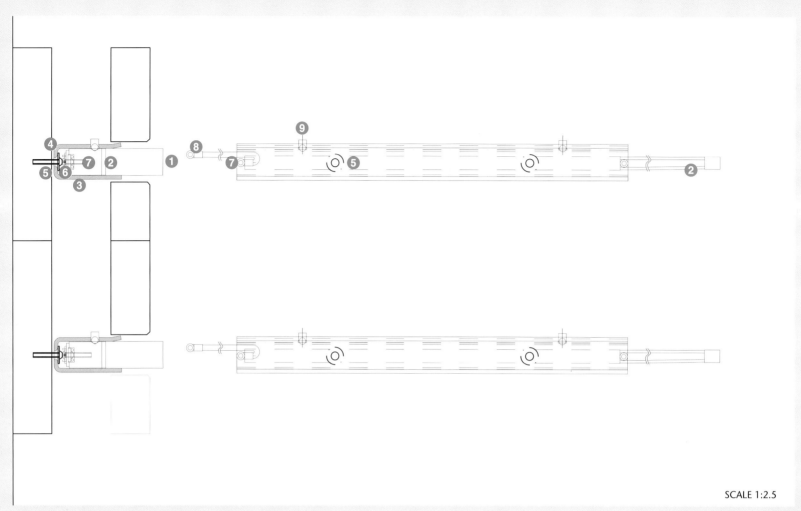

SCALE 1:2.5

OPPOSITE TOP
Section view of LED mounting detail
1 Clear acrylic lens (each section had to be cut at different angles to create a parallel surface and match the wall's mounting angle)
2 Opal lens
3 Mounting U-channel
4 Packing and mounting plate (allows for maximum 12-degree off-horizontal wall tilt)

5 M6 hole with M4 fixing and penny washer
6 LED and heat sink
7 Screw fixing of LED to acrylic lens
8 Safety lanyard
9 Ball spring plunger

BELOW
Section of wall showing variations in dimensions and angles which meant that each fitting had to be tailor-made to its location

BOTTOM
During the day, 70W ceramic metal halide, ground-recessed uplights accent the form and texture of the black wall (an effect mirrored by up/downlights on the textured limestone wall)

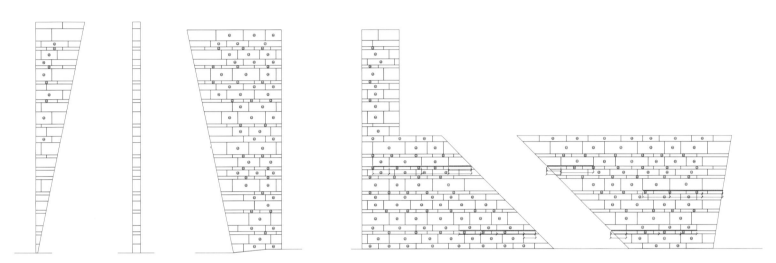

SCALE 1:150

13

SATELLITE 4, CHARLES DE GAULLE AIRPORT, PARIS
LIGHT CIBLES

Satellite 4 is the latest extension to Charles de Gaulle Airport, the second busiest airport in Europe and seventh in the world. Covering an area of 120,000sq m (1.2 million sq ft), the new building will be 756m (2,480ft) long, with two wings of 350 and 290m (1,150 and 950ft) in length, and have a passenger capacity of about seven million.

What is unusual about the ambient lighting in the circulation areas is that it is an integral part of the building rather than an added element. Specially designed by ADP and Light Cibles, the whole ceiling works as a lighting system. The false ceiling is made up of translucent plastic tubes, behind which high-efficiency 1.2m (4ft) linear T8 fluorescent tubes (36W 4000K) have been placed with an apparent randomness to provide general lighting, creating a soft, homogeneous illumination to the waiting, commercial and departure zones. The distribution of the light fixtures varies in density according to the function of the spaces, allowing illumination levels to be increased where appropriate without the need for additional downlights. The ceiling unit is around 50sq m (540sq ft) and has between six and 27 luminaires per unit.

The transparent tubes are ribbed inside, which multiplies the reflections created by the bare fluorescent lamps sitting above. The high specular aluminium reflector is an independent element separate from the luminaires, with two for every light fixture, producing a graphic effect of multiple images. The fittings also have an orientation function, with the continuous ceiling-recessed luminous paths marking the spaces and guiding the passengers through the circulation areas. The ambient lighting system is very efficient, producing an average 200 lux for less than 7W per square metre (10¾ square foot).

RIGHT
The key to the ambient lighting concept is that it is integral to the building rather than a separate element

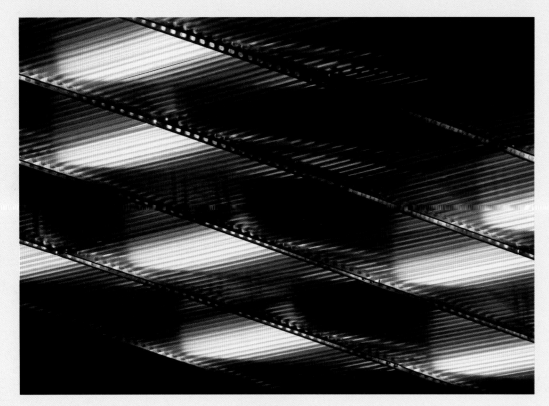

LEFT
The false ceiling comprises translucent plastic tubes, behind which are high-efficiency, warm white 1.2m (4ft) linear T8 fluorescent tubes

BELOW
Partial ceiling plan
The spacing of the light fixtures varies in density according to the nature of the space and the intensity of light level needed

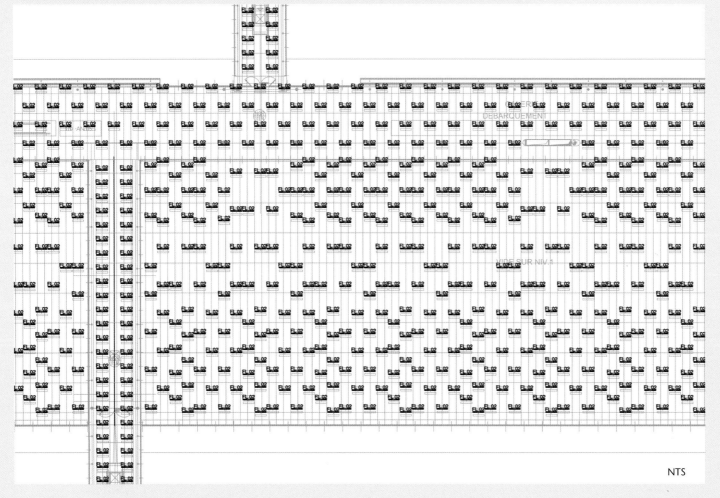

NTS

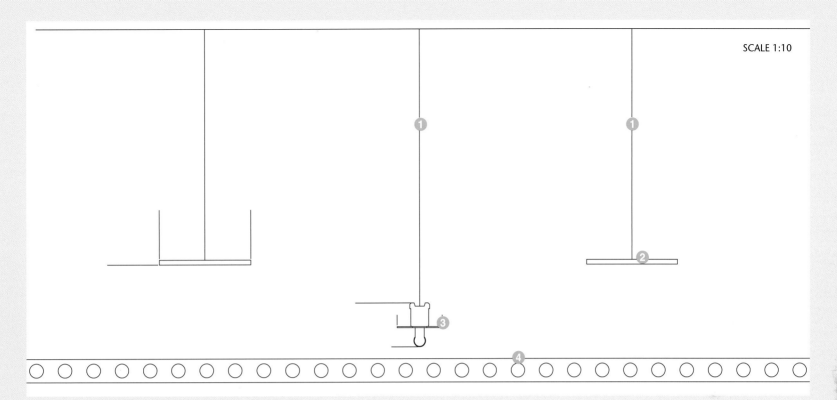

SCALE 1:10

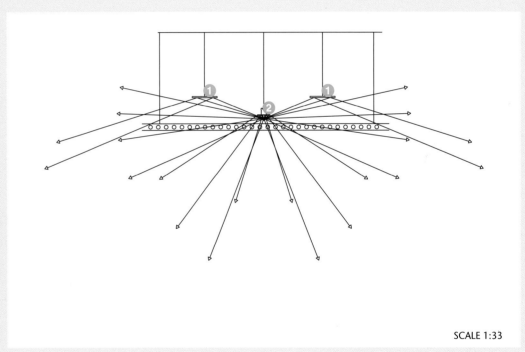

SCALE 1:33

TOP
Section detail of ceiling
1 Position can be adjusted according
  to the geometry of the tool bar to
  minimize light spill into the plenum
2 High specular aluminium reflector
3 Fluorescent fitting with reflector
4 Ceiling structure

ABOVE
Section detail of ceiling showing light
distribution
1 High specular aluminium reflectors
2 Fluorescent fitting

CAR PARK ONE, CHESAPEAKE ENERGY, OKLAHOMA CITY
ELLIOTT + ASSOCIATES

Poor quality light – often monochromatic sodium – is characteristic of most car parking spaces. The visual similarity of different levels and the difficulty of distinguishing colour means they can be disorientating, while little effort is made to help drivers recall the location of their vehicles.

These issues are all resolved in a fairly elementary but striking way for this corporate car park. Central to the concept is the idea of using colour, reinforced by coloured lighting, to help with orientation and for easy memorability. From the top, the floors are coded blue, green, yellow and red. Using a customized T8 linear fluorescent housing with direct and indirect components, the direct element provides white ambient light – a formed metal panel covers the source – while the gelled uplight gives the appropriate colour on the ceiling. Surfaces are painted white so that the interior acts as a giant reflector. Rather than a typical harsh, glaring light, the effect is luminous, continuous illumination.

The further introduction of a central atrium had a dual purpose: to bring natural light into the space and as an artistic element. Coloured T8 fittings are also run vertically either side of the atrium, changing colour according to the floor. Making colour an integral part of the lighting makes the space more understandable and memorable. It has also countered the usual sobriety associated with such a utilitarian environment – an unforeseen outcome is that people playfully select their floor according to the colour of their cars.

RIGHT
The simple device of putting gels on the uplight component of the fluorescent luminaires reinforces the colour coding for each storey

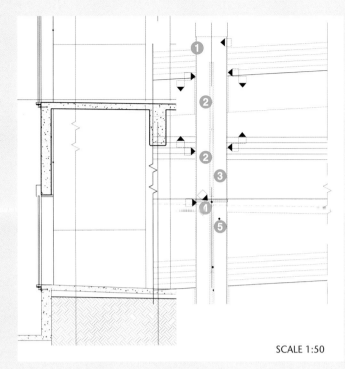

SCALE 1:50

ABOVE
Section view of second and third
atrium storeys
1 Column
2 Vertically mounted T8 fluorescents with
coloured tube guards matching interior
colour of each storey
3 Atrium face of column painted green
between horizontal chamfer elevation
marks for third and fourth storeys
4 Horizontal chamfer marks
5 Atrium face of column painted yellow
between horizontal chamfer elevation
marks for second and third storeys

ABOVE
The central atrium not only introduces
more daylight but allows the colour coding
to be turned into an artistic element

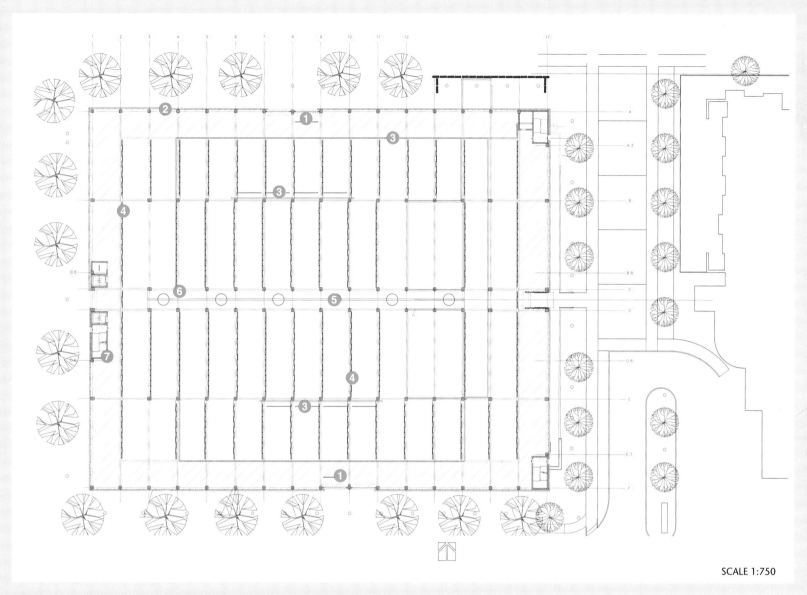

SCALE 1:750

ABOVE
Reflected ceiling plan (RCF) of first storey
1 Fluorescent wallwasher with cut-off visor
2 Stainless steel mesh painted black
  both sides
3 Fluorescent wallwasher
4 Single T8 fluorescent fitting, uplight
  element with coloured tube guard
5 Atrium open to sky
6 Fluorescent with coloured tube guard
  vertically mounted on column
7 Fluorescent with coloured tube guard
  in stairwell

CNIT, PARIS
LIGHT CIBLES

The emblematic CNIT (Centre of New Industries and Technologies) was one of the first buildings built in La Défense in Paris. A convention centre, it also houses a Hilton hotel and offices. The largest unsupported concrete span enclosed space in the world, its triangular structure, 50m (165ft) high at the centre of the roof, is supported on three points 218m (715ft) apart. A recent major refurbishment has increased the public space by reopening the lower floor, which now has new shops and restaurants.

The lighting scheme involved a number of strategic areas, including the inner space beneath the 50m (165ft)-high vaulted arch, for which the building is famous. Prior to refurbishment, this area was relatively dark and part of the strategy was to compensate for this lack of light. Around 600 racks of white LEDs are positioned at the base of serigraphically printed glass panels, creating dramatic luminous inner facade elements to lift the space.

As with the illumination of any glass form, glare was an issue and so an anti-glare profile in the form of a metal sheet – folded at 125 degrees and painted black on the inner surface – runs the length of each fitting. The fold hides the fixture, fixing elements and cables. On the second, third, fourth and fifth levels of the building, the linear system also has a trapezoid base, which allows for a generous angle of rotation and therefore precise positioning of both the fitting and anti-glare profile, according to the distance between the devices and the glass panels. On the ground floor, the fixture is recessed in the floor and integrated with a fluorescent lamp, while on the first floor there is no anti-glare profile as the light distribution is vertical.

RIGHT
Linear LED fixtures at the base of serigraphically printed glass panels are precisely positioned to glow without glare

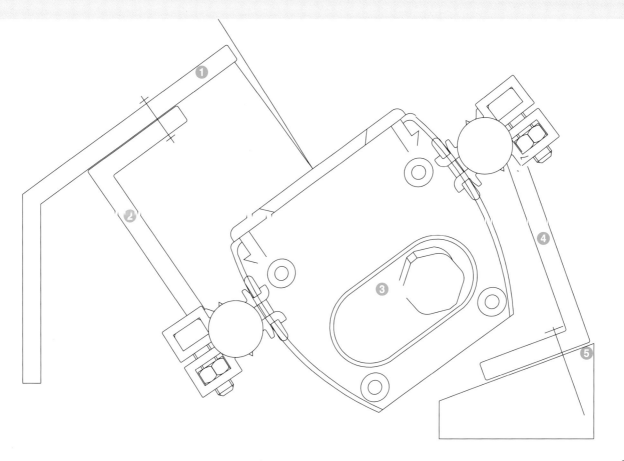

SCALE 1:1

ABOVE
Section detail showing installed fitting
1 Anti-glare profile, folded at 125 degrees
2 Fixing elements for the anti-glare profile
3 Linear LED fixture
4 Fixing stand
5 Trapezoid fixing base, allowing a large
rotation range for precise positioning

RIGHT
Fixing detail of the stand, 178mm
(7in) long

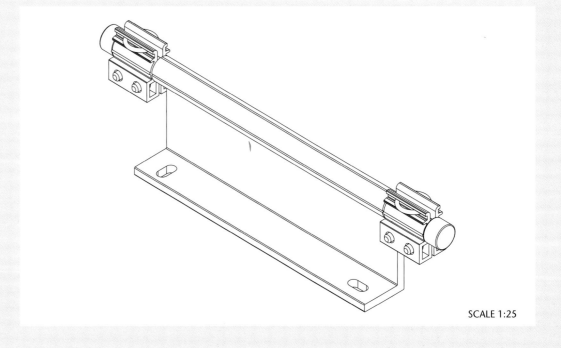

SCALE 1:25

LEFT AND ABOVE
The fittings create a diffuse luminous effect in a space that was formerly relatively dark

DELOITTE HQ, COPENHAGEN
STUDIO STEVEN SCOTT

Rarely does an artwork become an integral, organic part of an architectural structure as Steven Scott's colour-change installation does at management and financial consultant Deloitte's corporate headquarters in Copenhagen. On a massive scale – it is 26,000sq m (280,000sq ft) and extends seven storeys – it is a complex geometry of light and colour.

The aim here was to make the staircase element the central communications system, encouraging people to use the stairs even for higher floors. The imperceptibly slow shift in colours makes it the gently pulsating heart of the building. A total of 1,050 linear RGB LED strips, each 30cm (12in), are used under stairways and walkways, producing seven colours – violet, indigo, blue, green, yellow, amber and red. The predominant colour is white with another colour rising through it. With a vast skylight over the atrium and the transparency of the facades, a great deal of daylight can enter at different times of the year, so the interaction of daylight and artwork were critical to the choice of colours.

The light choreography is symbolic of people climbing the stairs and moving along walkways. Colours incrementally travel upwards in a clearly defined rhythm, pause momentarily to flood the walkways with light, then resume their upwards movement as a new colour composition begins to wind its way upwards. The programming, using a DMX controller, is based on the number seven. There are 77 spaces in all. When one field of colour has risen to space eight, space one is illuminated with another colour. The space eight colour then moves on to space 15. Then space one becomes the first colour again and the trio of colour moves up until the first field reaches space 22, and so it continues until space 77 is reached. That element of the process takes around 25 minutes, but for the whole stack to take on its colour needs three hours and 20 minutes, and 28 hours for the whole seven-colour sequence to be completed.

RIGHT
The LED installation extends seven storeys and is a complex geometry of light and colour

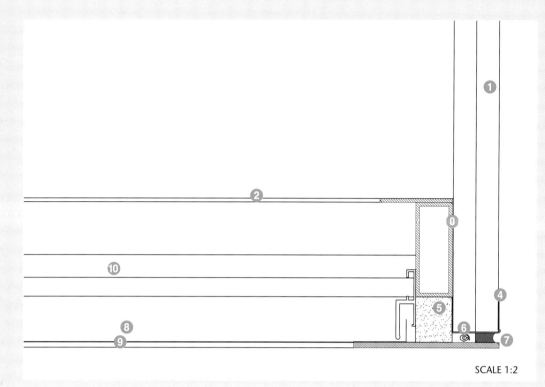

LEFT
Section detail of bridge
1 2 x 13mm (½in) plasterboards
2 Finished backing, painted
3 Profile edge of staircase
4 Edge rail
5 Fibre brick
6 Seal lining
7 Elastic sealant
8 Stretch ceiling
9 Newmat stretch ceiling fabric
10 LED housing

SCALE 1:2

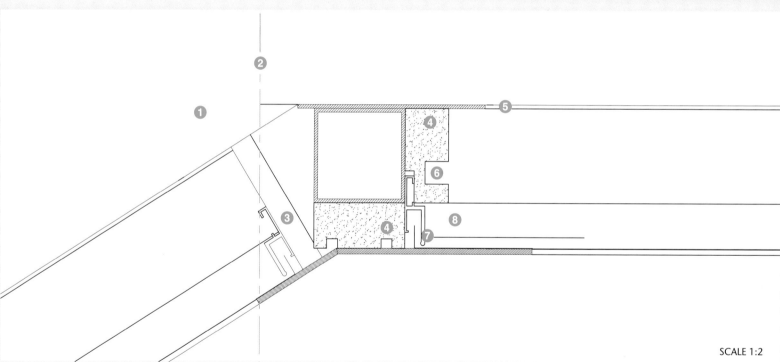

SCALE 1:2

ABOVE
Section detail of staircase
1 Stairs
2 Walkway
3 End piece
4 Fibre brick
5 Finished backing, painted
6 LED housing
7 Stretch ceiling
8 Cover

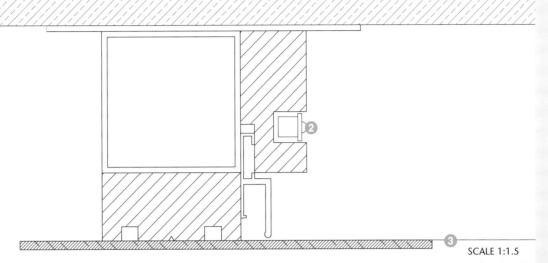

LEFT
Exploded section detail of stair
1 Underside of stair
2 RGB LED
3 Stretch ceiling

BELOW LEFT AND RIGHT
Seven colours incrementally travel upwards in a clearly defined rhythm, pausing to flood the walkways with light before resuming their upward movement. It takes 28 hours for the whole seven-colour sequence to be completed

SCALE 1:1.5

ENBW CITY,
STUTTGART
LICHT KUNST LICHT

The new office building complex for Germany's third largest power, gas and water supplier was designed as an exemplar of energy efficiency. It uses cutting edge building services to achieve this, including geothermal technology and underground water for heating and cooling. Lighting is a core part of this strategy and the aim was to reduce primary lighting energy consumption by 54 per cent compared to reference office buildings.

However, the aim was also to avoid utilitarianism. Applying daylight-linked control systems and efficient sources such as fluorescent, metal halide and LEDs, lighting is also used to create eye-catching elements to aid orientation. All aspects are exemplified by the treatment of the entrance lobby, and especially the two sculptural staircases that lie on either side of the reception desk. The desk is itself a focal point, with a luminous cloud – comprising layers of polished aluminum wire mesh and 400 open-distribution xenon sources – floating above it.

The central wall, to which the flights of stairs are attached, is clad in overlapping glass panels over which water flows. Between the panes are lighting profiles with narrow-beam LEDs aimed downwards, which suffuse the water with atmospheric grazing light. On the underside of the stairs a slender, warm white luminous strip (3500K T5 fluorescent lamps) traces the outline of the staircase and circumscribes the central water wall in a zigzag. The combined effect is a refreshing soft glow that draws the eye through the space.

The water flows into a large, shallow basin, which marks the boundary between the public part of the entrance hall and the internal part – a contemporary version of a moat delineated by LED illumination of the pool's edge.

ABOVE
The glowing water wall and the attached staircase sit behind and to the left of the reception, also a luminous focal point, drawing the eye through the space

BOTTOM LEFT
Positioning of LED profiles between glass panels over which water flows
1 Satinized glass panel, overlapping
2 Wall-mounted bracket
3 High-power IP68 LED profile, narrow beam, accessible for maintenance from one side
4 Stainless steel sheet with scalloped edge

OPPOSITE
A slender line of light on the underside traces the outline of the staircase, which itself wraps round the glowing water wall

BOTTOM RIGHT
Stair fitting detail
1 Stone plates in adhesive bed
2 Steel cover
3 Height adjustment
4 Light channel with overlapping T5 lamps.

SCALE 1:2

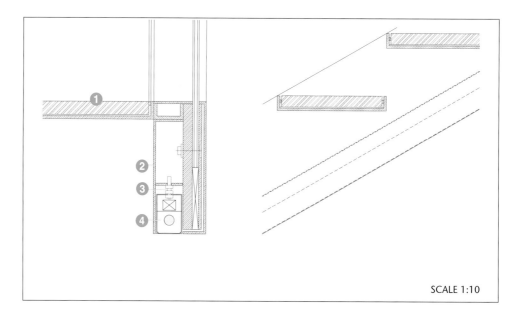

SCALE 1:10

GSC GROUP OFFICES, NEW YORK CITY
CLINE BETTRIDGE BERNSTEIN LIGHTING DESIGN

The design objective for the offices of this New York financial firm was to humanize a high-tech workplace with the look of an expensive boutique hotel. Dominating the space is an internally illuminated 205sq m (2,200sq ft) pixellated mural of Central Park that wraps around the core. A single row of low wattage, warm white LED wallwashers with a beam angle of 25 degrees is placed just behind the glass both at the bottom and top of each wall. The linear fixtures vary in length from 345mm to 1,345mm (13⅝in to 53in). Mounted at a 5-degree tilt, the LEDs light towards the core wall, which in turn illuminates the glass wall.

A particular challenge was to achieve an even illumination across the wall at the stairway where it rises a full two storeys. Close collaboration with the architect resulted in the creation of a cavity in front of the actual core wall to eliminate the interruption at the opaque spandrel level. Here two strips are placed at the floor of the lower level and two at the ceiling of the upper floor, while the additional fittings are fixed at a 2-degree angle so that the combination evenly lights the white wall behind the glass.

RIGHT
Wrapped around the core of the office space is a 250sq m (2,200sq ft) internally illuminated, pixellated mural of Central Park

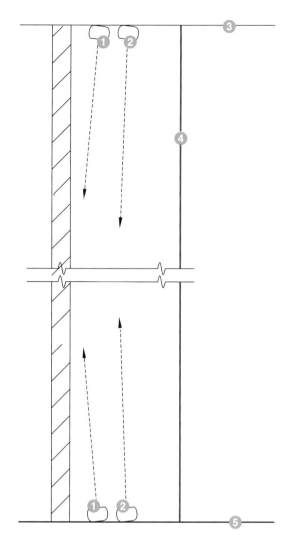

SCALE 1:12.5

ABOVE

The main challenge was to achieve even
illumination across the two-storey wall at
the stairway

ABOVE

Section of two-storey wall at stairway
1 Linear LED fitting with 5-degree tilt
2 Linear LED fitting with 2-degree tilt
3 Ceiling
4 Laminated glass panel
5 Floor

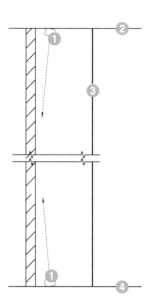

SCALE 1:25

ABOVE
Section of single-storey wall
1 Linear LED fitting with 5-degree tilt
2 Ceiling
3 Laminated glass panel
4 Floor

ABOVE RIGHT
The glowing green mural is balanced with carefully controlled white light composition. In the boardroom, three lines of fluorescent light (for activities such as video conferencing) are punctuated by MR16 LV tungsten halogen spots for a more residential feel

RIGHT
Fixture mounting detail
1 Steel angle bracket
2 LED linear fixture
3 GWB partition
4 Printed vellum graphics adhered to glass
5 Access panels

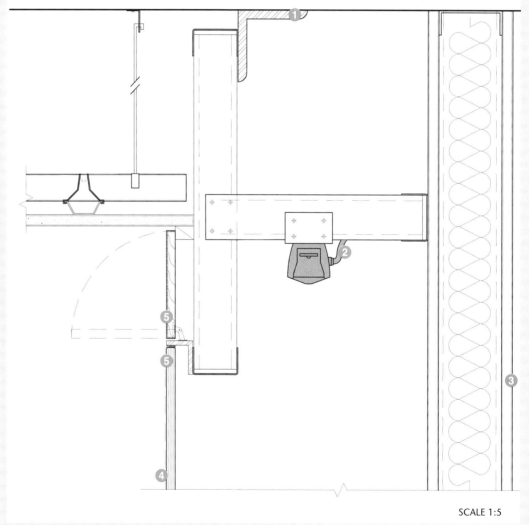

SCALE 1:5

KPMG HQ, LONDON
LIGHT BUREAU

The lighting brief throughout KPMG's new City HQ was for a low-energy but sophisticated lighting solution that would reinforce brand identity and a sense of openness – the building has few internal barriers, allowing clients and staff to mix and mingle on all floors.

The light sculpture, located in the ground-level reception, was intended both to enhance the double-height space and also as a visual metaphor for the interconnectivity of the company's business. Positioned above a seating area, it lowers the perceived height, mitigating the empty volume above, but still maintains the views to the mezzanine.

While the sculpture is unique, the components are essentially standard luminaires, Artemide Kao linear T5 fluorescent pendants. Made of white-painted aluminium with a polycarbonate diffuser, each luminaire comprises pre-assembled and pre-wired sub-units which can be put together in any configuration. The electrical connections are made by quick connectors. Stainless steel support cables have grip-lock connectors for height adjustment.

The sculpture has a total of 15 luminaires using 42 14W and 28W warm white (3000K) lamps. The installed load is 840W, although operationally they are dimmed, on Dali ballasts, to about 50 per cent output. Overall the structure measures 44m (144½ft) long, 20m (65½ft) high and 14m (46ft) wide, with a weight of 12kg (26½lb).

RIGHT
The low-energy light sculpture in the reception exploits the double-height space and acts as a corporate metaphor

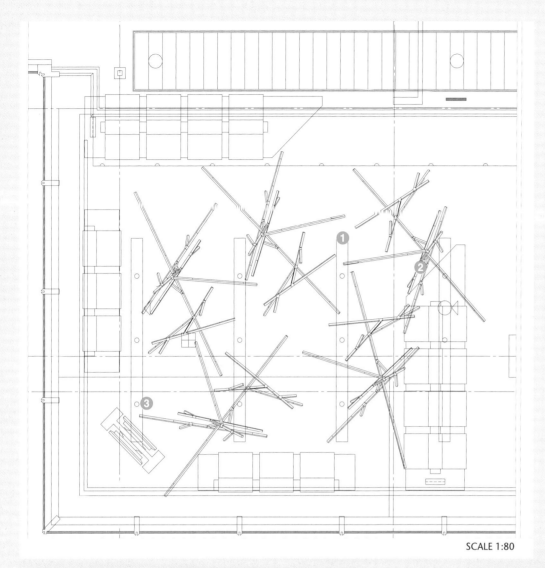

SCALE 1:80

LEFT
Plan view
1 Wire suspension points to avoid downlight troughs
2 Cluster of pendants located to allow Genie lift access to downlights above
3 Sections/arms with lamps to be rotated (using 3D modelling) to provide illuminated views from mezzanine above and ground floor below

BELOW
While the configuration is unique, the components are standard T5 luminaires

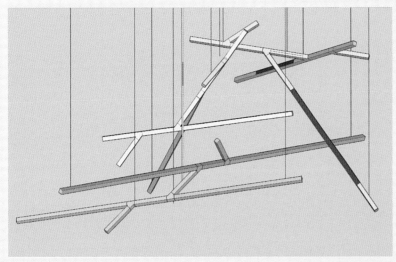

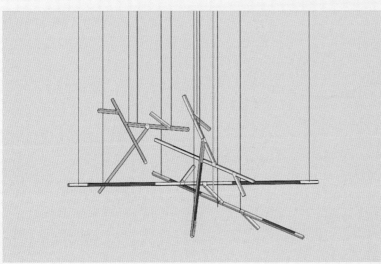

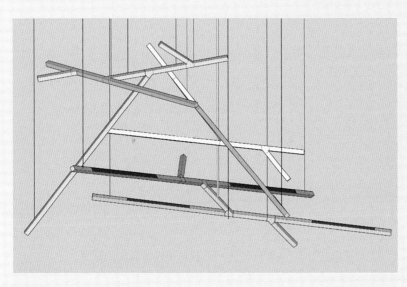

TOP AND BOTTOM
Visuals showing section and plan views of the sculpture, which is also visible from mezzanine level

ABOVE
The three types of luminaire clusters which were then grouped to form the sculpture

CONVENTION/BANQUETING FACILITY, QATAR NATIONAL CONVENTION CENTRE, DOHA
LIGHT + DESIGN ASSOCIATES

The Oyster, which makes reference to Qatar's history of pearl cultivation, was specially developed not only as a light source but as a crucial element in changing the perception of the venue from a 4,500-seat convention hall into a 2,000-seat 'intimate' banqueting facility for heads of state and other dignitaries. Part of Qatar's landmark 15 million sq m (160 million sq ft) Education City, the Qatar National Convention Centre (QNCC) is itself vast – 100 x 100 x 16m (330 x 330 x 52½ft). Designed by Arata Isozaki, the QNCC houses ten auditoria, providing world-class education and performance facilities.

When the hall is in use as a convention venue, the 28 fittings – 1.5m (5ft) diameter in closed state – are parked at ceiling level where they can be lit in any colour or dynamically change colour, operating individually or in sequences. When the hall changes use to a banqueting facility, they slowly lower and open up to reveal a 5m (16½ft) span of crystal glass panels backlit with colour-changing LEDs.

The Oysters are orchestrated by a closed-loop control network with ACN logic linked to the production lighting systems. They can drop individually or in sequences to create a dramatic light ballet, eventually collectively forming a lower ceiling height of 3.2m (10½ft). The entire process had to be achieved within very stringent noise criteria and, due to the airflow patterns set up by the air conditioning systems, there also had to be no visible horizontal movement in each fixture when at their lowest position and fully extended.

RIGHT
The Oyster acts as both lighting and architectural element, opening up and descending to a height of 3.2m (10½ft) to create a more intimate feel when the space switches from convention hall to banqueting facility

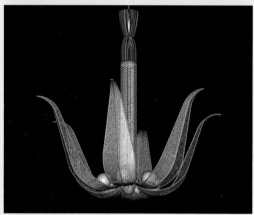

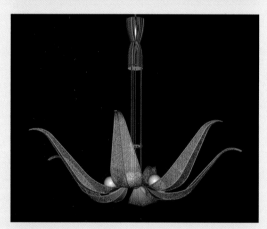

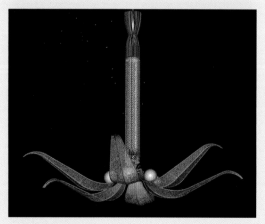

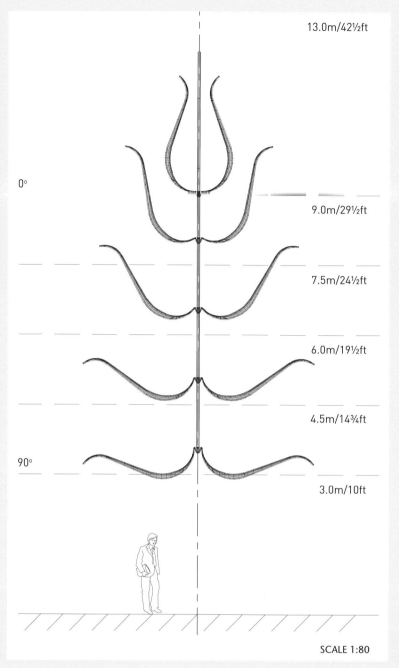

13.0m/42½ft

0°

9.0m/29½ft

7.5m/24½ft

6.0m/19½ft

4.5m/14¾ft

90°

3.0m/10ft

SCALE 1:80

LEFT, TOP TO BOTTOM
As the Oyster descends from its 16m (52½ft) closed parking position it gradually opens (60 seconds), a function that can be choreographed to music as the fittings drop individually or in sequence

ABOVE
Section view showing dimensions of the fitting at various stages of descent

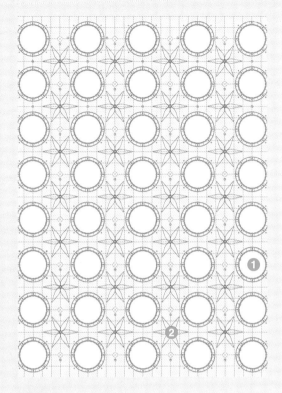

ABOVE
Part RCP of convention/banqueting facility
1 Barrisol elements backlit with
colour-changing LEDs
2 Oyster fitting, open position

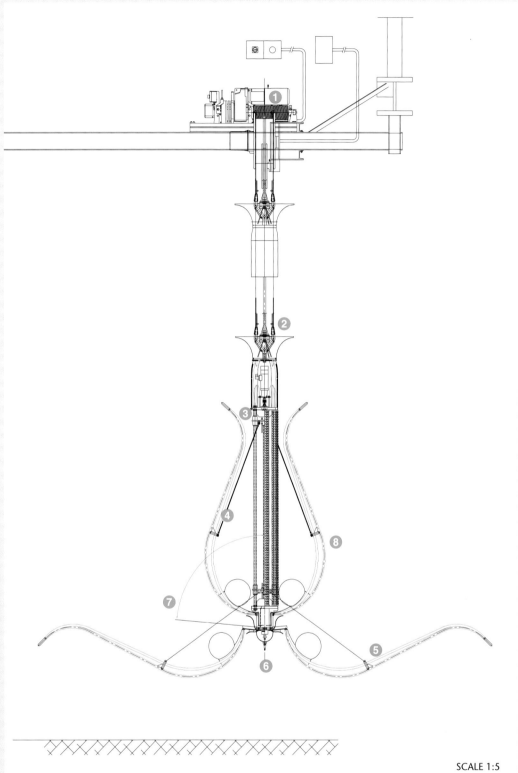

SCALE 1:5

ABOVE
Section view
1 Winch and cable management system
2 Fixing frame
3 Carriage
4 Crystal glass panel (x 6)
5 LED illumination (x 6)
6 Pivot system
7 Pivoting range
8 Leaf

PALACE OF INTERNATIONAL FORUMS, TASHKENT
PFARRÉ LIGHTING DESIGN

Clad entirely in marble on a base of black polished granite, the Palace of International Forums makes a grand statement in the heart of the Uzbekistan capital. Designed for events and international conferences, it has two extensive foyers, one for government and one for public use, a 1,850-seat auditorium, conference rooms and a banquet hall.

The lighting remit covered both exterior and interior (28,000sq m/ 300,000sq ft), and necessarily reflected the grandiose ambitions of the setting. Where possible lighting was integrated but the scheme also involved specially designing and manufacturing a large number of chandeliers and luminaires. In all 1.8 million crystals and more than a quarter of a million LEDs, alongside metal halide, halogen and fluorescent lamps, were specified for a total 9,400 light points.

One of the most ambitious installations is the series of 12 LED rings, six located in each of the two grand VIP staircases. Suspended from a height of 24m (78¾ft) and falling to 3.4m (11ft) above the floor, the largest is 5.5m (18ft) in diameter and the smallest 2.5m (8ft), with the weight ranging from 220kg to 450kg (485lb to 990lb). The custom-made aluminium H-profiles are secured with narrow (just 20mm/¾in) polished stainless steel tubes. Clad on both sides with three million rhinestones, the inner and outer circles glow with light from warm white (3000K) LEDs behind a patterned acrylic diffuser. There are 40,000 LEDs in total using 20kW.

Echoing the motif are customized circular wall lights. These are housed in a recessed opening with a custom-made gypsum surround, which melds them into the stucco lustro wall surface. The central 120cm (47¼in)-diameter disc is aluminium with a matt white finish, which creates a corona effect. The fitting uses eight 24W TC-L fluorescent lamps.

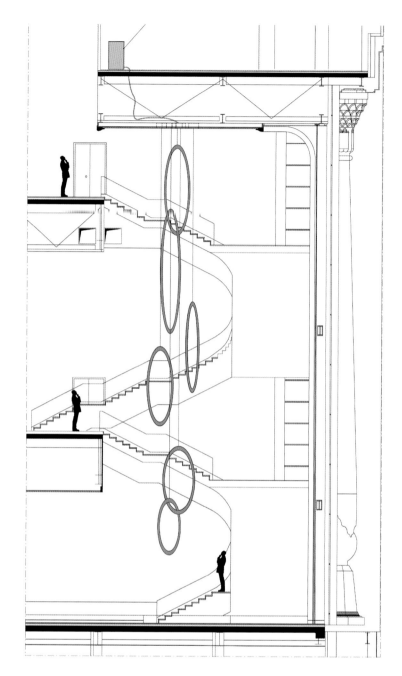

SCALE 1:150

ABOVE RIGHT
Section of one stairway with LED ring lights suspended through three storeys

OPPOSITE
The rings are clad on both sides with three million rhinestones, while the inner and outer circles glow with light from warm white LEDs behind a patterned acrylic diffuser

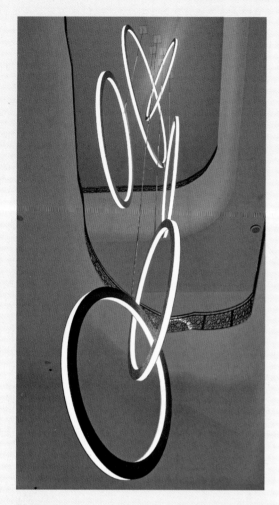

ABOVE
Suspended from a height of 24m (78¾ft),
the largest ring is 5.5m (18ft) in diameter
and the smallest 2.5m (8ft)

RIGHT
Cross section of H-profile ring light
1 Structured polycarbonate cover
2 Warm white (3000K) LEDs
3 Screw channel
4 Aluminium reflector
5 LED girder section profile with
  aluminium cooling ribs
6 Strass crystals (both sides)

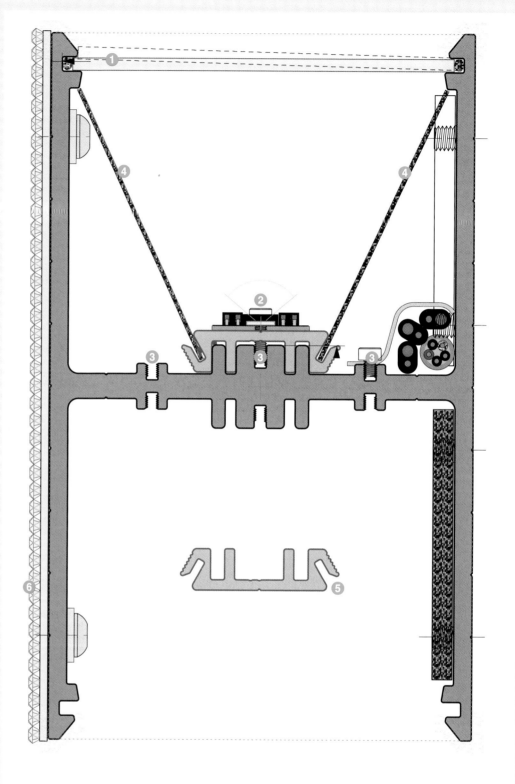

SCALE 1:1

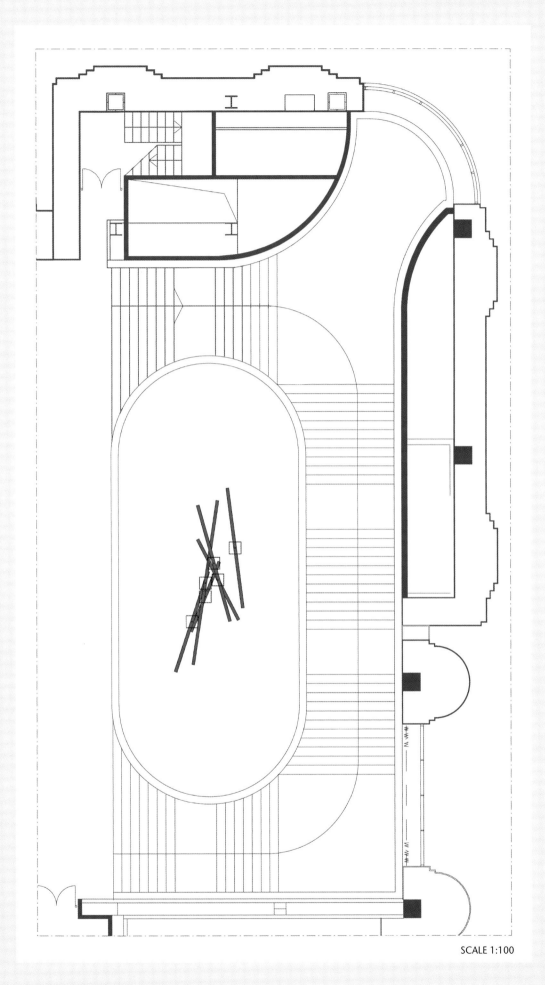

LEFT
Plan view of one stairway showing
configuration of rings

SCALE 1:100

ASSEMBLY HALL, LIECHTENSTEIN PARLIAMENT
LICHT KUNST LICHT

The assembly hall, with its distinctive 18m (60ft)-tall pitched yellow brick roof, sits above a columned hall on the ground floor of architect Hansjörg Göritz's new parliament building. The dominant feature of the space is the specially made 9m (30ft) chandelier, which mirrors the ring-shaped table below. The concept of the chandelier evolved for pragmatic reasons. The original solution of a series of small pendants was rejected in favour of a structure that would not only light the space, but also discreetly house the cameras and microphones necessary for online coverage.

For functional reasons, there had to be sufficient horizontal illuminance levels on the table as well as appropriate vertical, highly uniform illuminance levels for shadow-free facial recognition. Accent lighting was also needed to model the space. The chandelier therefore has both directional and diffuse lighting components, each concealed behind a bronze fabric upholstered to a frame and forming the bottom edge of the luminaire ring. The individual fabric panels can be removed for maintenance.

Altogether the ring holds 36 compact fluorescent lamps, 72 halogen lamps, eight microphones and four dome cameras, all of which had to be wired inconspicuously. The solution lay in grouping the cables into 12 bundles. Each strand is threaded through a 20mm (¾in) tubular profile from which the chandelier is suspended. Without visible canopies and attachments, the profiles disappear between the bricks of the roof slope.

RIGHT
The imposing 9m (30ft) chandelier neatly houses microphones and cameras, and provides diffuse and directional lighting

ABOVE
Showing the directional lighting on (left)
and off (right), and how panels can easily
be removed for maintenance

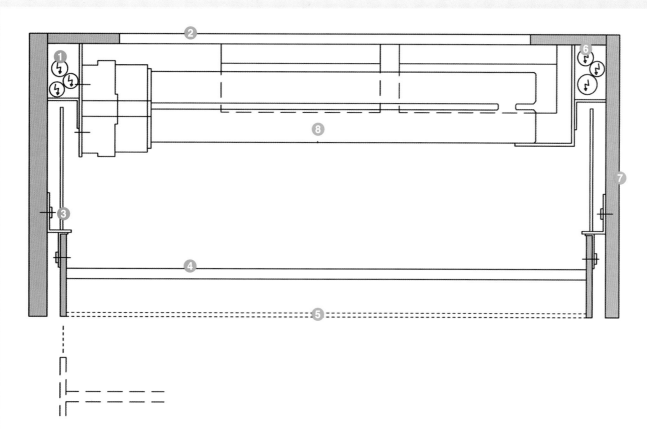

LEFT
Detail section of
chandelier showing
diffuse light component
1 Electrical feed for lamp
2 Acrylic glass (clear)
3 Spring clamp
4 Acrylic glass (frosted)
5 Tin-bronze mesh
6 Data cable, media etc.
7 Luminaire housing
8 18W TC-L lamp

SCALE 1:1

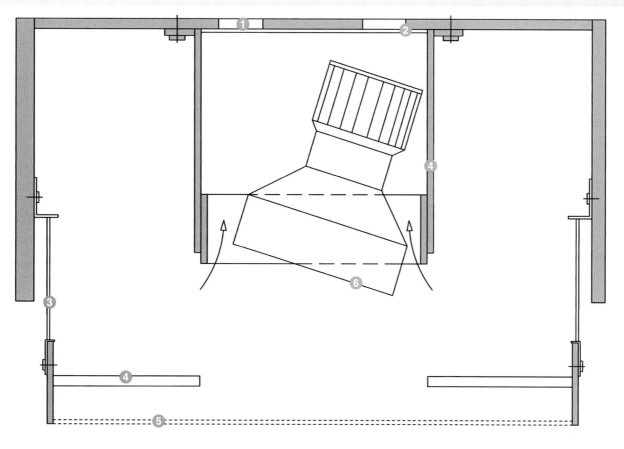

LEFT
Detail section of
chandelier showing
directional light
component
1 Ventilation
2 Bronze gauze
3 Spring clamp
4 Acrylic glass (frosted)
5 Tin-bronze mesh
6 Gimbal projector with
50W QT12 lamp

SCALE 1:1

ROPEMAKER PLACE, LONDON
ARUP ASSOCIATES, ZUMTOBEL LIGHTING, SAS INTERNATIONAL, STORTFORD INTERIORS

Specially designed for the entrance foyer of a BREEAM Excellent-rated City of London office development, the ceiling system combines both a direct/indirect lighting source and acoustic baffling. The system also had to fulfil a number of other criteria. First, it had to create an impact as the principal feature of the 10.5m (34½ft)-high corner foyer. Second, it had to provide a visual focus when viewed from outside. Third, it had to form both the main internal ceiling surface and the external canopy surface, so that there was visual continuity between the interior and exterior.

The eventual solution of a sculptural, waveform-shaped ceiling was designed by Arup Associates in collaboration with lighting manufacturer Zumtobel, SAS International and Stortford Interiors. The series of illuminated vaulted waves flow into the interior, so that the volume of the space appears expanded by the uplit waveform surfaces. The pre-formed white PPC micro-perforated steel sheeting has a white tissue interlayer and an acoustic blanket, together with a clear acrylic diffuser which contains the individually addressable linear fluorescent luminaires. The fact that fittings can be controlled independently allows the light across the space to be exactly balanced.

The high-output, low-glare diffuser is a bespoke linear extrusion that uses Zumtobel's patented waveguide technology. This refracts a proportion of the light on to the ceiling and the remainder into the interior. The relationship between the diffused refracting light source and reflective surfaces, together with its profile, were determined through extensive mock-ups which iteratively refined the design. The individual ceiling cassettes were based on a 1,500mm (59in) module (actually 1,475mm/58in), and designed to exactly fit a standard linear fluorescent luminaire to make construction and replacement easier.

RIGHT
Specially designed for the building's entrance foyer, the ceiling system combines direct/indirect lighting and acoustic baffling

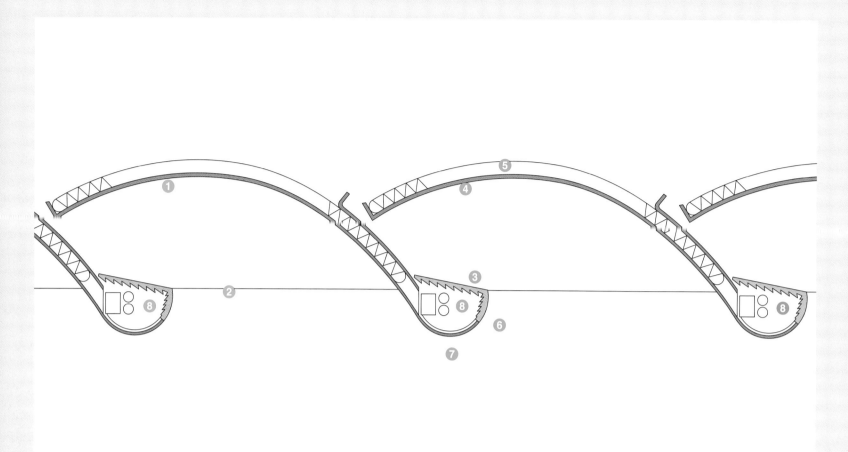

SCALE 1:10

ABOVE
Section detail of waveform ceiling
1 Perforation omitted for exterior section
2 Line of bulkhead or flat ceiling portion
3 Fresnel lens cover as dust cover and
even light distributor
4 16 per cent perforated curved reflector
with white tissue interlayer and RAL
9010 20 per cent gloss finish
5 Acoustic blanket
6 Half quadrant Fresnel lens to light
opposite lower section
7 Single linear perforation to provide
accent sparkle to lower section
8 T5 fluorescent lamps

LEFT
The bespoke linear extrusion refracts a
proportion of the light on to the ceiling
and the remainder into the interior

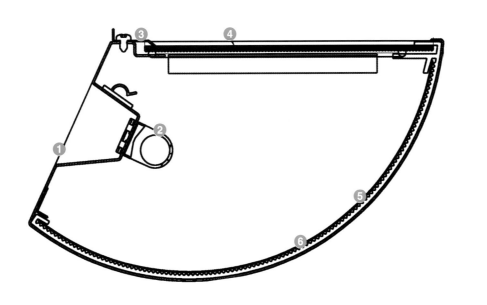

SCALE 1:2

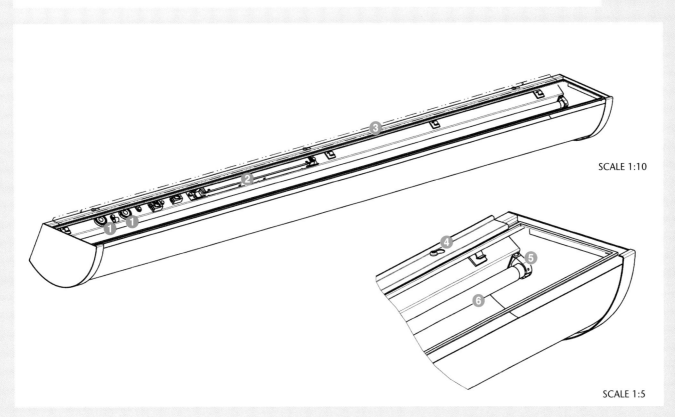

SCALE 1:10

SCALE 1:5

PLATFORM 5, SUNDERLAND STATION
JASON BRUGES STUDIO

Passengers waiting on the platforms of Sunderland railway station face a 144m (472½ft)-long, 3m (10ft)-high glass-block wall which divides the area from a disused platform behind. This wall has now been transformed into a large, low-resolution video matrix (755 x 15 pixels), which conjures up shadowy figures who also appear to be waiting for their trains behind the glass. The animated figures each display different behaviours – friends stand together in conversation, others bring their dogs or read newspapers – based on the movements of 35 local people who were filmed acting as typical passengers. Their movements were digitally deconstructed and then reassembled to create the animations on the light wall. Simple sensors register the motion and location of trains, and a control system combines this information with the character behaviour to produce the moving figures.

The installation uses warm white LEDs, designed to create a comforting contrast, especially in winter months, with the cool white fluorescents used for the architectural lighting. A monochromatic palette and carefully controlled animations ensure the installation is not too distracting for train drivers. Special mounting frames were designed for the lighting so that all maintenance can be carried out at floor level and behind the wall rather than trackside.

RIGHT
Waiting passengers watch shadowy figures who appear to be standing on the deserted train platform behind a glass-block wall

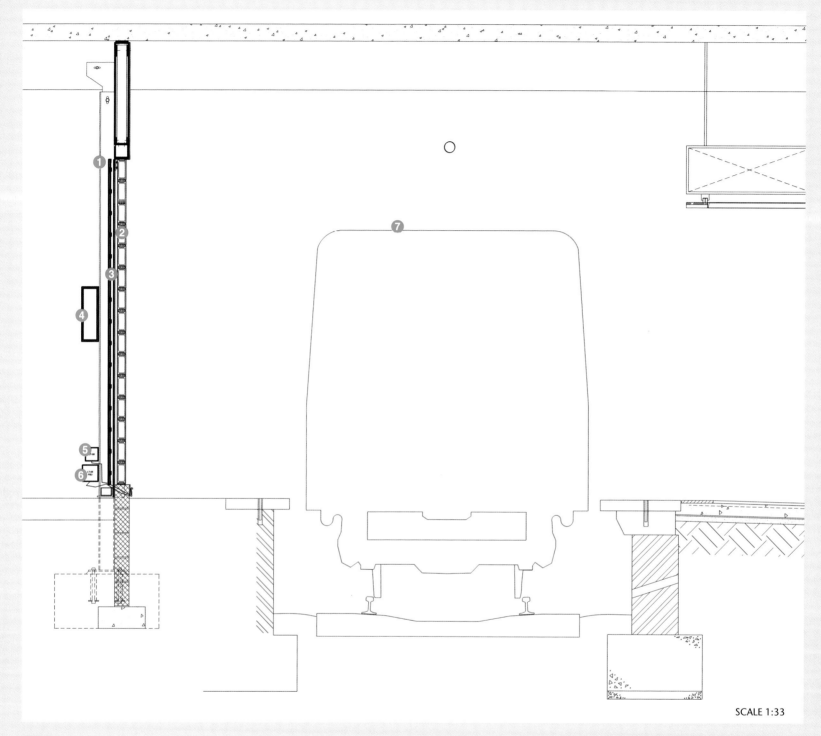

SCALE 1:33

ABOVE

1 Windpost

2 Glass-block light wall

3 LED festoon system in strands of 15 LED nodes mounted on custom thick mild steel frame

4 LED driver supplying eight strings of luminaires, and 16-port gigabit speed Ethernet Layer 2 network switch

5 RS232 to TCP/IP convertor for transmitting sensor data back to computer via the lighting control network

6 Power supply to train position and movement sensor with data output for connection to computer

7 Train

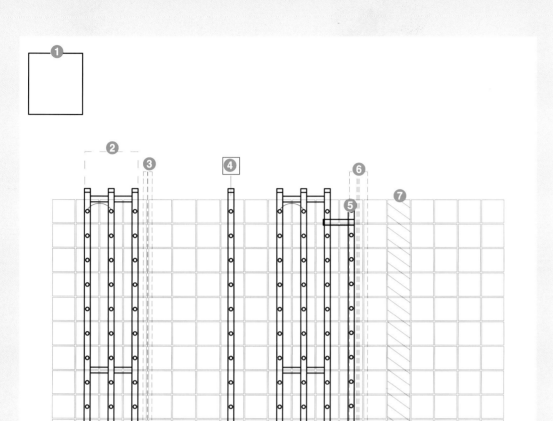

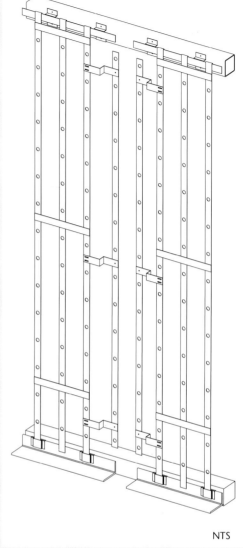

NTS

NTS

ABOVE

Detail of video matrix
1 LED driver supplying eight strings
  of luminaires
2 Triple mounting frame (45 nodes)
3 T-section
4 Single mounting frame (15 nodes)
5 Short single mounting frame (15 nodes)
6 Wind post
7 Glass blocks fully obstructed by
  wind post

ABOVE

Detail of custom mounting frame for
LED luminaires made from 2mm ($^1/_{12}$in)-
thick mild steel, with a matt-black
powder-coated finish

PARTHENON GALLERY,
ACROPOLIS MUSEUM, ATHENS
ARUP

The exploitation of light, both natural and artificial, is central to the architectural design of the Acropolis Museum, and is exemplified by the treatment of the Parthenon Gallery. Conservation was not an issue with most of the exhibits and allowing daylight to enter the building created the outdoor conditions in which the sculptures and statues would have been viewed originally.

Adopting principles commonly found in the theatre, the daylighting strategy involves continuous linear skylights, which allow daylight from above to graze down the sculptures. This adds a dramatic effect to the otherwise flat light from the side windows, enhancing the modelling effects by day.

Arriving at this particular solution – creating optimal daylighting and viewing conditions, while maintaining good thermal and visual comfort – involved extensive testing of different window and rooflight configurations as well as modelling the effects of different daylight scenarios on the displays.

While daylight is the principal light source during the day, the artificial illumination, including two-temperature fluorescent ambient lighting, has been designed to complement the natural source by responding to the diurnal changes through automatic dimming. Accent light comes from tungsten halogen spotlights that are integrated with the skylights so that the visual clutter on the ceiling is minimized and the flow of light always emanates from the same point on the ceiling.

Warm white fluorescent wallwashers are surface mounted in the trough to even out shadowing. The Parthenon frieze is made up of original pieces sitting alongside new pieces, which have been made in a different material to ensure that they are clearly identified. Under daylighting conditions the whole frieze is illuminated, but under artificial light only the original pieces are lit (using additional spotlights with elliptical lenses), reinforcing their status.

ABOVE
Daylight is controlled by treated, double-glass glazing and is balanced with artificial light according to the time of day and natural light levels

RIGHT
1 Wallwash fittings (55W 3000K PL fluorescent) mounted in trough
2 Accent lighting from track-mounted spots (3000K tungsten halogen) aimed at right angles to enhance the sculptural qualities of the frieze
3 Diffuse daylight through the skylights
4 Filtered daylight through double-glass skin, screenprinted shading treatment
5 Dual-colour temperature fluorescents for ambient lighting

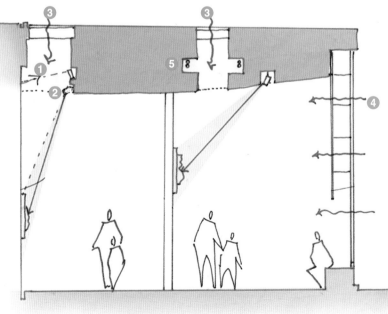

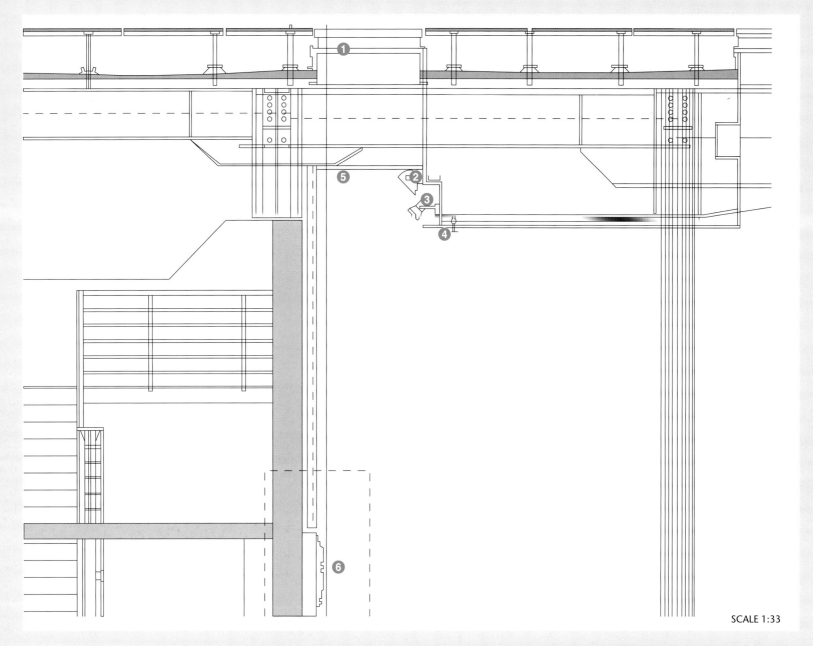

SCALE 1:33

ABOVE
Section view showing lighting to frieze
1 Double-glass layer skylight
2 Surface-mounted wallwashers
  every 1.5m (5ft)
3 Track-mounted spotlights every
  0.75m (2½ft)
4 Acoustic ceiling panels
5 Fabric diffuser
6 Parthenon frieze

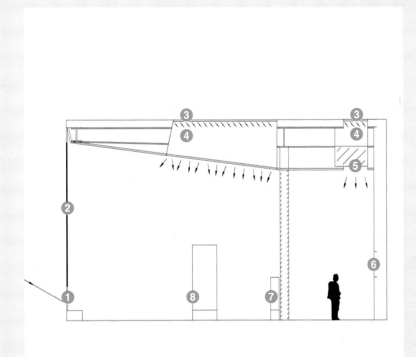

SCALE 1:12.5

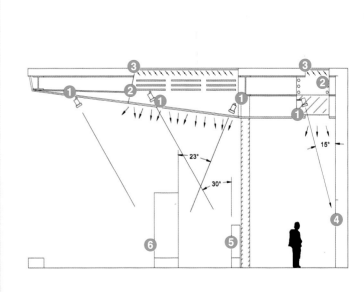

SCALE 1:12.5

Skylight, sidelight, daylight and integrated electric options were studied for all four facades. Shown are the studies for the east and west elevations

ABOVE
Sectional study of skylight and sidelight option that was selected for east and west facades
1 Clear
2 Fritted glazing with varying density
3 Adjustable louvres
4 Skylight
5 Transverse baffles
6 Parthenon frieze
7 Metope
8 Pediment

ABOVE RIGHT
Sectional study of integrated electric and daylight scheme that was selected for east and west facades
1 Tungsten halogen spotlighting
2 Dual-colour temperature fluorescent lamps
3 Adjustable louvres
4 Parthenon frieze
5 Metope
6 Pediment

CHAGALL'S AMERICA WINDOWS, ART INSTITUTE OF CHICAGO
LUX POPULI AND
VINCI HAMP ARCHITECTS

The renovation and reinstallation of the America Windows at the Art Institute of Chicago involved their relocation from their original position against windows into an interior space against a wall. However, the pieces had been designed to be viewed under natural light, so it was crucial that this effect was simulated convincingly. A key aim, for instance, was to avoid the typical impression from lightboxes of the lack of depth behind the image. Other important factors were conservation, presentation and maintenance access. Extensive studies, tests and modelling were used to resolve a series of challenges.

Behind the glass triptych is a simple grid of cool white (4100K) 32W T8 fluorescent tubes spaced 16cm (6in) apart. The light needed to be diffused into a uniform field, but while this can be easily achieved by attaching milk or opal acrylic to the back of the stained glass, it flattens the look of the glass and removes the perception of depth. Rigid elements would have also made maintenance access more problematic. Experimentation showed that two sheer curtains of different densities gave an ideal result: the absolute minimum density of diffusion required to conceal the lighting, but retain the sense of depth.

Ventilation of the lighting and maintaining a constant temperature (irrespective of time of day and dimming levels) were vital to avoid cracking the glass and lacquers. The fixtures behind are mounted to an uninsulated west-facing exterior wall of an old building, so there was thermal variation from the building. The fluorescent lamps heat the volume during the day so forced ventilation is necessary to cool it. Radiators switch on outside lighting hours to prevent the box cooling in winter. As there was no space for supply ducts, the step in front of the piece (recreated from the original location) is an air outlet, but that solution led to the issue of light leakage. This was resolved by making the step a series of offset baffles (like a car muffler), giving airflow a free path, but forcing light to bounce off matt black surfaces at least seven, but an average of 30 times, before leaking out the front.

To avoid edge effects (where lightboxes shift in character slightly as the viewer looks towards the edges), instead of the traditional matt white-painted side walls, they are mirrored. With opposing mirrors, the lighting appears to be infinite behind the glass.

RIGHT
Backlighting is a common technique but in this case required an exacting process that precisely recreated the effect of natural light from a window while considering conservation, maintenance and other issues. Chagall ®/© ADAGP, Paris and DACS, London 2011

THE MODERN WING, ART INSTITUTE OF CHICAGO
ARUP AND RENZO PIANO BUILDING WORKSHOP (RPBW)

The Modern Wing at the Art Institute of Chicago is a 24,620sq m (265,000sq ft), three-storey extension to the existing landmark museum and a collaborative effort between Renzo Piano Building Workshop (RPBW) and the lighting studio at Arup. The use and manipulation of daylight plays a key role, in particular the 4,200sq m (45,200sq ft) 'flying carpet', a highly detailed passive daylight system. Located above the new galleries on the third floor, it allows them to be illuminated with generous but controlled amounts of natural light that meet conservation limits. In addition to providing solar shading, its primary function is to filter and diffuse daylight before it passes into these top-lit galleries.

The system comprises 3,000 white, extruded-aluminium cantilevered 600mm (23½in) blades, each roughly 4m (13ft) long. Sculpted and shaped for structural stability they sit at a precise angle. The angled blades are open to the north to allow in diffuse skylight and to block southern sun, while low angle sun from the east and west is blocked by a series of fins attached to the blades.

Supported at two anchor points, the blades are fixed by castings to a triple-layer steel girder grille made out of composite welded box sections. There are three overlapping grilles with different profile and screen widths. Connections are completely hidden in the hollow steel boxes, which gives a flawless appearance from outside. Cables for the lighting are concealed in the profiles.

The system took ten years to develop and refine with extensive computer modelling and testing, including full-scale mock-ups. It works in tandem with photocells and a lighting control system, finely calibrated to adjust the electric lighting to fluctuations in daylighting levels according to time of day, season and weather.

ABOVE RIGHT
The 4200sq m (45,200sq ft) 'flying carpet' is a passive daylight system that sits above the new galleries on the third floor

RIGHT
Using photocells and a finely calibrated lighting control system, the electric lighting adjusts to fluctuations in daylighting levels according to time of day, season and weather

OPPOSITE
The system allows galleries to be illuminated with generous but controlled amounts of natural light that meet conservation limits

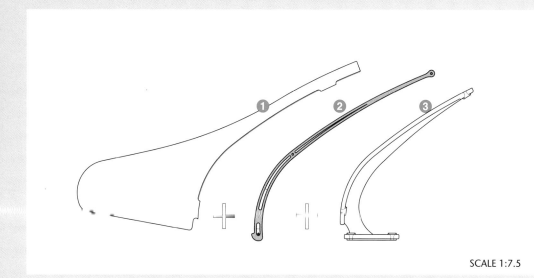

SCALE 1:7.5

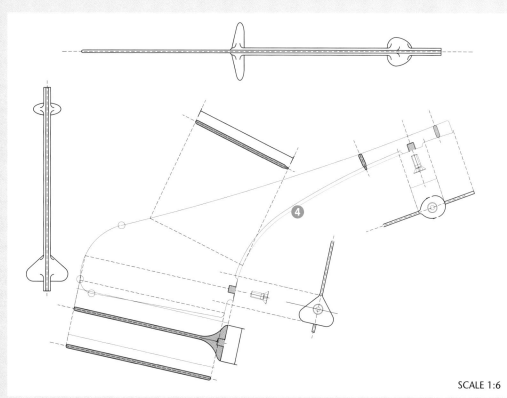

SCALE 1:6

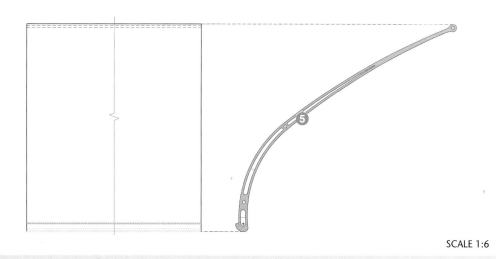

SCALE 1:6

LEFT
The three components of the flying carpet
1 Fin
2 Blade
3 Bracket

CENTRE
4 One of 21,000 cast-aluminium fins that protect the gallery from early morning and late afternoon summer sunlight penetration

BOTTOM
5 One of the 3,000 extruded aluminium blades, each around 4m (13ft) long, that protect the gallery from southern sun. The blade angle of 50 degrees was carefully selected to regulate daylight transmission into the gallery below

OPPOSITE CENTRE
Section detail of the flying carpet looking west
1 'Flying carpet' support structure, known as cassettes
2 Secondary steel structure
3 Tertiary steel structure
4 Primary steel structure. All structural elements were rounded at the bottom to maximize light transmission and minimize visual impact from below

OPPOSITE BOTTOM LEFT
1 Cast-aluminium bracket connecting blade and fins to the supporting structure
2 Connection to support structure

OPPOSITE BOTTOM RIGHT
1 At the end of each blade is a special 'shadow flap', a modified fin to close the gap between adjacent blades, ensuring the sun does not leak through the gaps needed to allow for tolerance and movement
2 Standard fin

ABOVE

Supported at two anchor points, the blades are fixed by castings to a triple-layer steel girder grille made of composite welded box sections

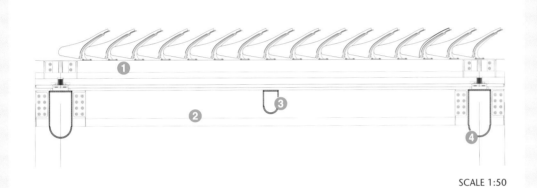

SCALE 1:50

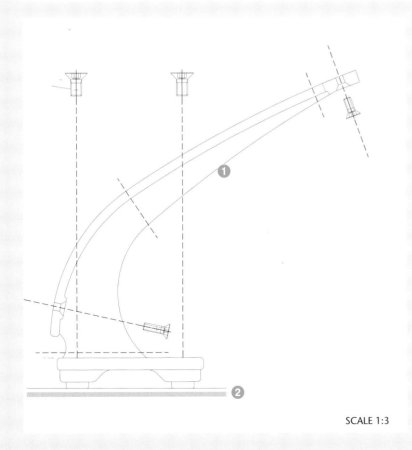

SCALE 1:3

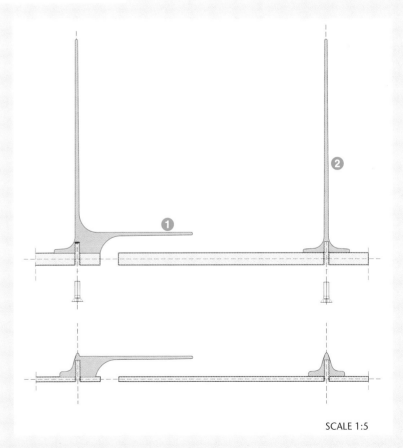

SCALE 1:5

BRIDGE PAVILION, ZARAGOZA
BARTENBACH LICHTLABOR

Designed for Expo 2008 in Spain, Zaha Hadid's structure is both exhibition pavilion and link between the main train station of Zaragoza (Saragossa) and the Expo site. Spanning 270m (886ft) across the Ebro River, the two-level bridge comprises four intersecting elements and a ramp which travels its length.

The primary concern for the lighting was to address the tunnel effect of the bridge. The sense of claustrophobia was countered with a careful selection of different light intensities. Natural light enters through the scaly facade to produce a pleasant dappling effect, but artificial lighting both supplements daylight and provides the sole illumination in other spaces. The interaction between light, materials, surface textures and architecture was extremely important.

Metal halide downlights and integrated linear fluorescent form part of the scheme, but the main ambient light comes from a mix of metal halide and halogen spotlights. Invisible to visitors, these are integrated into the wall cladding between the structural ribs and balustrades of the bridge, directing glare-free light upwards into the apex of the bridge. Here an integrated reflector band made from varnished aluminium runs along the entire length, changing from convex to concave according to the height, evenly illuminating the area with secondary light.

The luminaires respond to the time of day and the different levels of natural light available, using a Dali-based dimming system. During daylight hours, only the bright, cool white metal halide fittings are used. Towards the evening the halogen fittings come on, gradually reaching full output and blending with the metal halide luminaires to warm up the scene before it switches solely to halogen light at night.

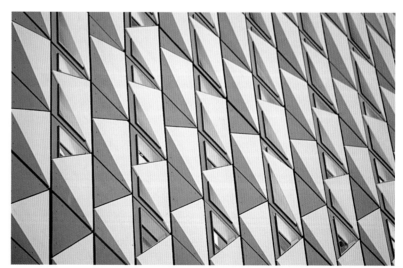

TOP
The main concern for the lighting was to counter the potentially claustrophobic effect of the 270m (886ft)-long interior.

MIDDLE AND BOTTOM
The 'scales' and openings in the facade allow natural light to fall into the main thoroughfares, but also allow the interior light to shine out at night.

OPPOSITE
An integrated varnished aluminium reflector band runs along the entire length, changing from convex to concave according to the height, evenly illuminating the area with secondary light.

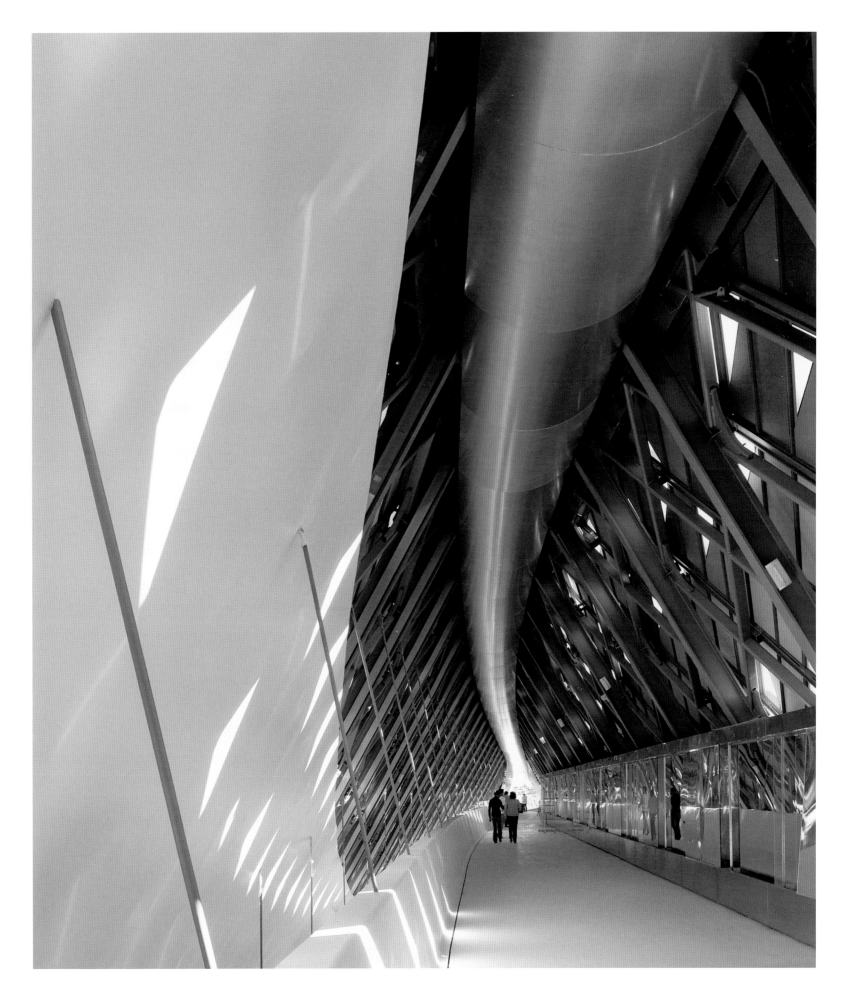

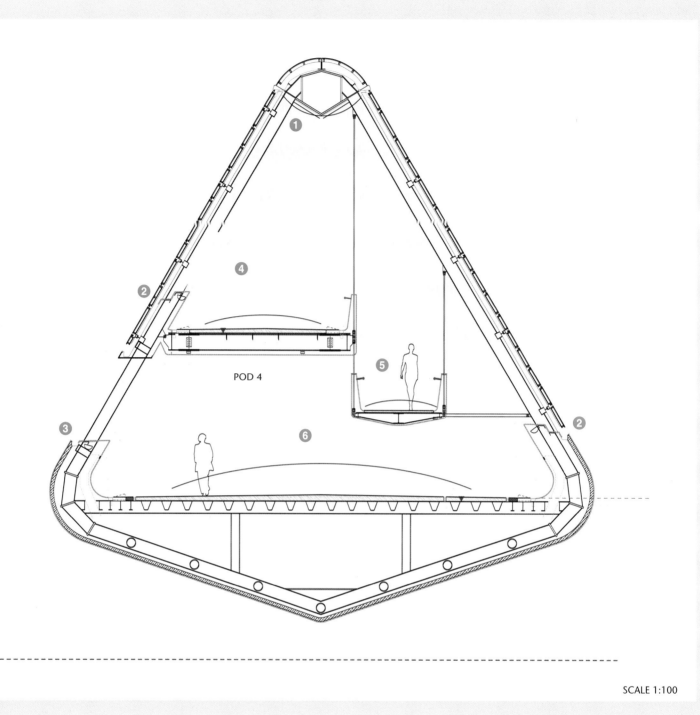

POD 4

SCALE 1:100

ABOVE
Cross section of Pod 4
1 Aluminium reflector in apex of bridge
2 Spotlight (alternating halogen and metal halide)
3 Parallel light: direct, extremely narrow-beam fluorescent fitting to provide a wallwashing effect
4, 5, 6 Horizontal illuminance

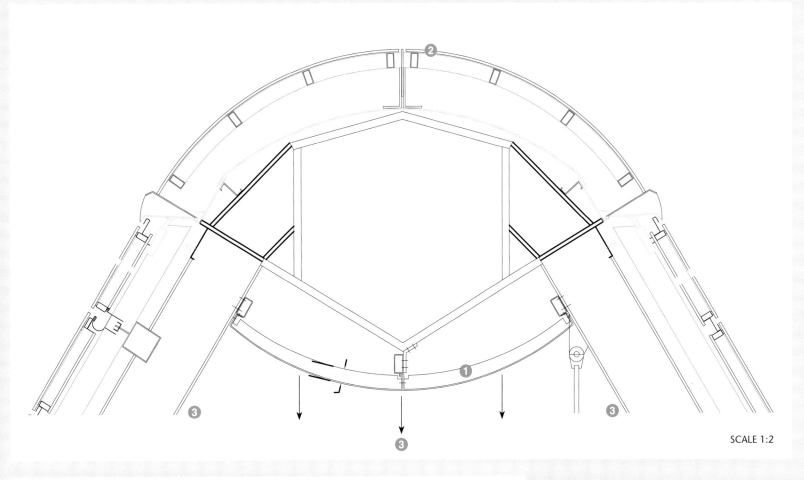

SCALE 1:2

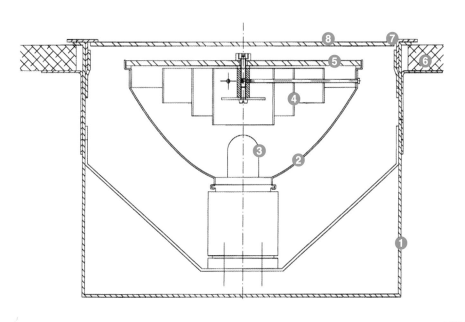

SCALE 1:3

ABOVE

Section showing convex reflector at apex (the integrated reflector runs along the entire length, changing from convex to concave according to the height)

1 Convex reflector made of highly reflectant aluminium

2 Apex of roof structure

3 Even secondary light distribution from metal halide and tungsten halogen spotlights in the wall cladding below directed up at the reflector

LEFT

Dali-controlled pivotable 150W low-voltage tungsten halogen spotlight

1 IP54 installation housing

2 Reflector

3 Light source: 150W 24V tungsten halogen

4 Anti-glare surfaces with shading device

5 Clear glass cover

6 Cladding

7 Cover

8 Closing glass with UV filter

THE COOPER UNION, NEW YORK CITY
HORTON LEES BROGDEN LIGHTING DESIGN

The nine-storey vertical campus at the Cooper Union for the Advancement of Science and Art in Manhattan brings together its schools of engineering, art and sciences, previously housed in separate buildings. Designed by Morphosis Architects, it has achieved an LEED Platinum green building rating, the highest possible. Its powerful forms reflect the cross-disciplinary elements of the institution, forging together art and engineering.

At the core of the building is the full-height atrium and sculptural 6m (20ft)-wide grand staircase which rises four storeys, wrapped in an undulating lattice of glassfibre-reinforced gypsum. The dynamism of the structure reflects the importance of these spaces as an area for communication, a vertical piazza encouraging casual but creative encounters, especially between the disciplines. Lifts in this connective space stop only at every third floor ('skip stop'), so that both students and faculty are positively encouraged to interact with each other.

Lighting in these spaces is more randomized, breaking free of the highly structured approach elsewhere. The atrium/grand stair are characterized by an intense luminosity. The primary illumination comes from translucent, backlit fibreglass at the skip stop bridges. Fluorescent (T8 3500K) surface-mounted striplights integrated into the curling rail structure illuminate the fibreglass, which wraps around one entire side as well as the bottom of each bridge, creating a compelling visual effect.

The complexity of the structure and the need to avoid glare made the additional, general lighting of the space a challenge. The solution lay in a carefully focused array of shielded filament 35W ceramic metal halide (R-111) fittings directed towards the smooth surface of the atrium's north wall. The reflected warm light (3000K) from the 40-degree beam fittings fills the volume and indirectly illuminates both the stair below and the flowing net-like surround, offering glare-free viewing through the many portals created by the architecture. Adjacent circulation corridors were purposefully kept relatively dark to enhance the juxtaposition of light within the structure and the surroundings.

ABOVE
Providing glare-free lighting to the complex lattice structure enveloping the staircase was achieved with reflected light from shielded metal halide fittings

OPPOSITE
The intense luminosity of the grand staircase comes from fluorescent fittings integrated into the curving handrail, which illuminate the translucent fibreglass

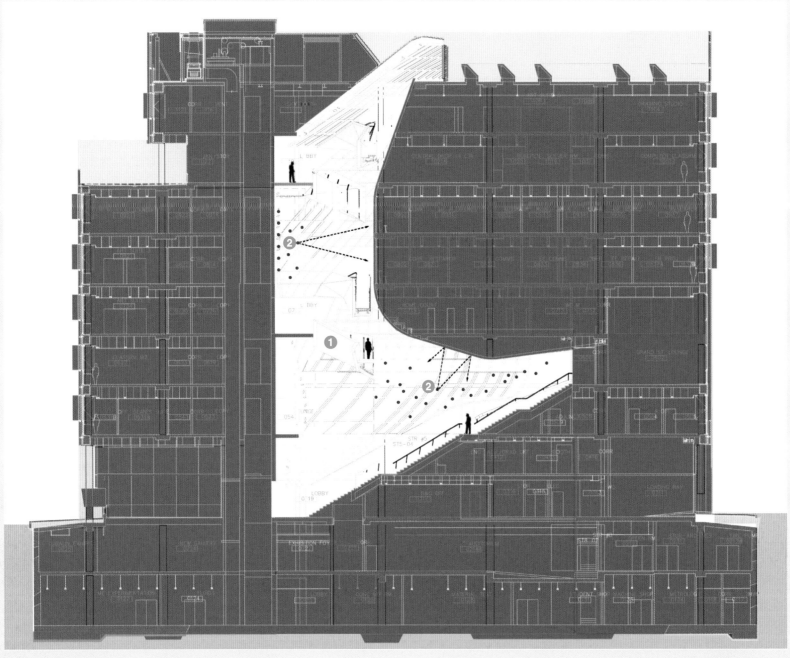

ABOVE
Building section
1 Luminous resin rail lights stairs and
  upper volume
2 Shielded metal halide accents highlight
  the architectural 'belly' and reflect back
  to light the lower stair

RIGHT
Section and plan views of shielded
filament spotlights providing reflected
ambient light
1 Wall
2 Metal halide lamp ballast
3 Spotlight
4 35W ceramic metal halide R111 lamp
5 Wall
6 Junction box
7 Canopy

SCALE 1:7.5

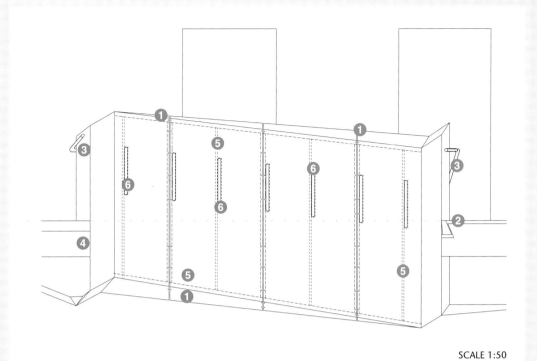

LEFT
Resin rail detail
1 Resin panel with galvanized steel tube structure
2 Concrete fill over metal panel
3 Primed painted pipe
4 Structural concrete slab
5 Steel tube structure
6 The 0.6m (2ft) fluorescent striplight is set a consistent distance (around 0.3m/12in) from the top edge of the rail

SCALE 1:50

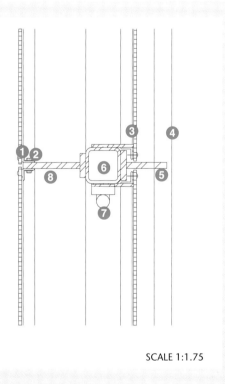

SCALE 1:1.75

ABOVE
Resin stair rail with integrated fluorescent striplighting
1 Exposed fasteners with gasket spacer
2 Angle frame enclosure structure
3 Resin panel attached to angle frame
4 Stainless steel handrail
5 Steel plate handrail support
6 Steel tube structure
7 Linear fluorescent fitting attached to structure
8 Steel plate handrail support

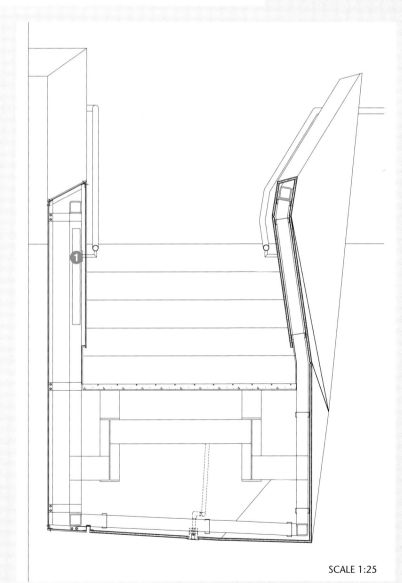

LEFT
Stair section at landing
1 The striplight in the rail allows ease of access for maintenance from the stair side. Light passes through the resin to light the stair and bounces within the resin cavity to softly light the resin below the treads

SCALE 1:25

THE LIGHTCATCHER, WHATCOM MUSEUM, WASHINGTON
CANDELA

The Lightcatcher at the Whatcom Museum is a 3900 sq m (42,000sq ft) regional art and children's museum. It takes its name from its most visible feature, the lightcatcher, a multifunctional translucent structure that reflects and transmits sunlight. The gently curving, sandwich-glazed wall, 11m (36ft) high and 55m (180ft) long, has a frosted outside panel and amber fritted inside panel. It sweeps through the building at the physical centre of the project, bounding a 650sq m (7,000sq ft) exterior courtyard, while forming a glowing interface between the museum's interior and exterior spaces. With integral fluorescent lamps to create a glowing lantern at night – the courtyard is designed as a civic gathering space – it is intended to celebrate the play of light.

During daylight hours, the light-porous wall acts as an energy-saving light fixture, gathering natural light and transmitting it into the interior as a warm glow, providing ambient and exhibit lighting. It also helps ventilate the building; its double-glazed skin acts to keep interior spaces cool using the stack effect. In cooler weather, vents at the top of the wall can be closed and radiant energy is captured within, insulating the building.

Reflectored, double-lamp T8 fluorescent strips (selected rather than T5 because there was less of a heat issue when they were sleeved) sit at the base of the wall between the glass panels. Structural elements within the wall were barriers to light penetration but also provided opportunities for revealing interesting patterns and textures. Salmon and yellow sleeves on separately switched lamps provide either rich depth of colour with the structural elements picking up both shades, or a single intense colour fading up the wall. Roof-mounted metal halide floodlights with changeable coloured lenses provide deep and variable colour to the top portion of the wall. Barn doors and baffled snouts restrict light spill. Access panels at the base allow easy maintenance of light sources from the interior. The wall is highly energy efficient using just 0.2W per 0.09sq m (1 sq ft).

At dusk, interior halogen lights, mounted on track integrated into the wood-slat ceiling, accent artwork while the deep blue sky blends with the salmon/yellow light inside the wall. After dark, halogen track lights illuminate the glass wall, providing reflected ambient light. Using a daylight-linked control system, accent lights illuminating the artwork increase in apparent contrast as the daylight disappears.

RIGHT
The curving, translucent wall reflects and transmits sunlight during the day. At night integrated fluorescent lamps transform it into a lantern

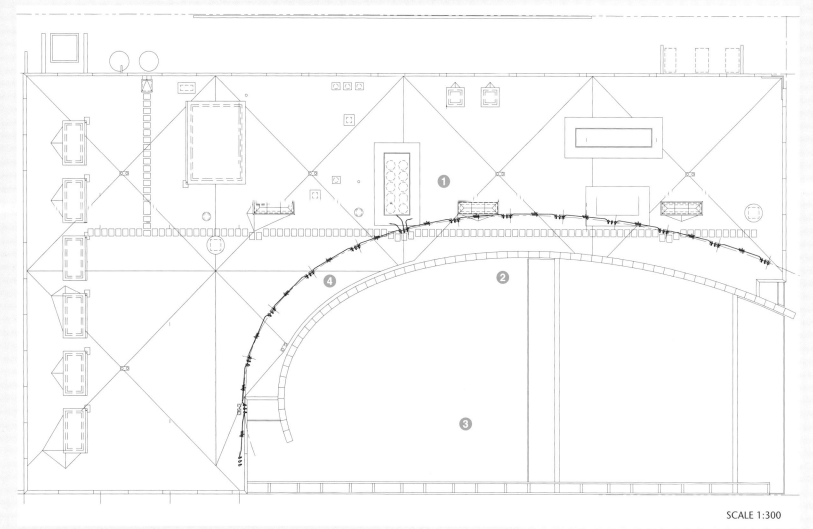

SCALE 1:300

ABOVE
Plan view of the Lightcatcher wing
of the museum
1 Galleries
2 Glass wall with fluorescent fittings
   at the base
3 Exterior courtyard
4 Roof-mounted floodlights to
   illuminate top of wall

LEFT
The wall slices through the physical
centre of the project, a glowing interface
between the museum's interior and
exterior spaces

LEFT
During the day, the light-porous wall acts as an energy-saving light fixture, gathering natural light and transmitting it into the interior, providing ambient and exhibit lighting

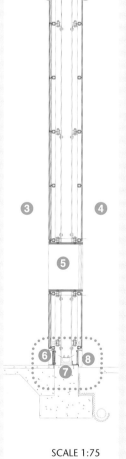

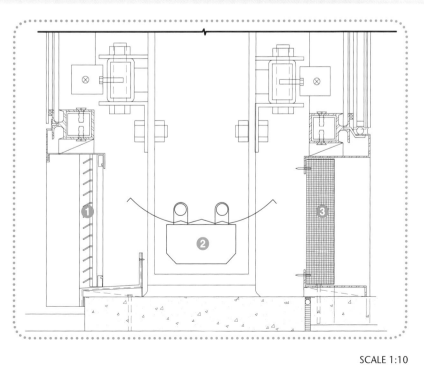

FAR LEFT
Section of glass wall
1 Insulated glazing
2 Glazing
3 Gallery
4 Exterior courtyard
5 Aluminium jamb beyond
6 Removable insulated aluminium panel
7 Fluorescent light fitting
8 Vent

LEFT
Section of glass wall base
1 Removable insulated aluminium panel
2 Fluorescent light fitting
3 Vent

SCALE 1:75

SCALE 1:10

RENÉE AND HENRY SEGERSTROM CONCERT HALL, COSTA MESA, CA
CLINE BETTRIDGE BERNSTEIN LIGHTING DESIGN

Imposing but not dominating, the subtle spiral form that fills the impressive volume of this concert hall foyer perfectly expresses the soft curves of the space. It comprises 300 stainless steel stems, which vary in length from around 15cm to 11m (18in to 36ft), increasing in 3.5cm (1³/₈in) increments to create the 12m (40ft)-diameter spiral. Each one culminates in a stainless steel housing and crystal diffuser with a central cavity, custom made by Baccarat. The housing contains a 1W white (3000K) LED. Because the rods are so slender – each is less than 1cm (³/₈in) in diameter – the effect is of floating dots of light.

The stems, each with a 'hang straight' fitting, are suspended from a ceiling mounting plate, aluminium to match the ceiling finish, which is aluminum leaf. Californian regulations required that the chandelier was earthquake proof so there is a discreet system of sway bracing (0.5cm/¹/₅in diameter) between the stems. The LED drivers are housed in the ceiling where they are accessible from above.

The chandelier's context completes the overall effect. The centre of the ceiling above is studded with a spiral of Swarovski crystals, backlit by fibre optics with both colour-change and twinkle-effect wheels. The crystals are specially silver tipped at the bottom so that they reflect light back on to the ceiling. Around the spiral are apertures with ceramic metal halide framing projectors. These are specialist designed to illuminate a very precise area, in this case the 'circle of honour' on the lowest of the four balconies, where the names of donors are etched into the thick, back-painted dichroic glass.

The ceiling cove on the top balcony is lit with fibre optics, using a metal halide lamp and colour-change wheel. The two balconies in between this and the circle of honour are lit by white LEDs set between two acrylic blades with sand-blasted ends (the only part visible) set into the balcony front. These are different depths – the top is around 12cm (4¾in) and bottom around 9cm (3½in), offset from each other. The LEDs illuminate the inside of the box rather than the blades themselves, creating an even light rather than appearing as a row of dots.

ABOVE
The 300 stainless steel stems culminate in a Baccarat crystal diffuser housing a 1W white LED

OPPOSITE
All lighting effects are achieved with efficient LEDs and metal halide, using even less energy than stipulated by California's stringent Title 24 codes

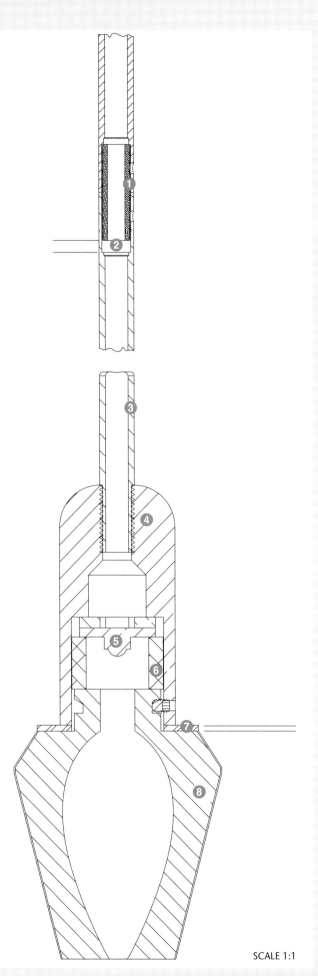

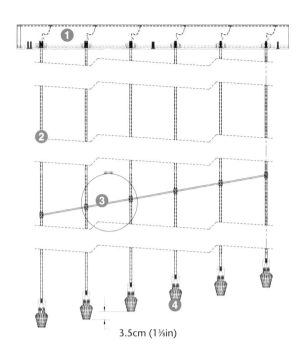

3.5cm (1⅜in)

SCALE 1:20

LEFT

Section of chandelier detail. Optimum light distribution proved to be from a conical-shaped crystal with a hole in the middle

1 Internal coupler
2 Extra thread, allowing a good connection for internal coupler joining stem segments internally
3 Polished stainless steel rod (less than 1cm/³/₈in)
4 Polished stainless steel housing
5 1W warm white (3000K) Nichia LED
6 Heat sink/spacer
7 Stainless steel disc to give finished look when viewed from above
8 Hand-blown Baccarat crystal diffuser

ABOVE

Detail of chandelier components

1 Decorative cover plate over ceiling mounting, aluminium to match aluminium leaf ceiling finish. Behind is a recessed continuous channel. Multiple fixtures are wired to one LED driver located above the ceiling for access
2 Stainless steel rods, less than 1cm (³/₈in) in diameter and varying in length from 45cm (18in) to 11m (36ft)
3 0.5cm (¹/₈in) sway bracing
4 Crystal diffusers with 1W white LED

SCALE 1:1

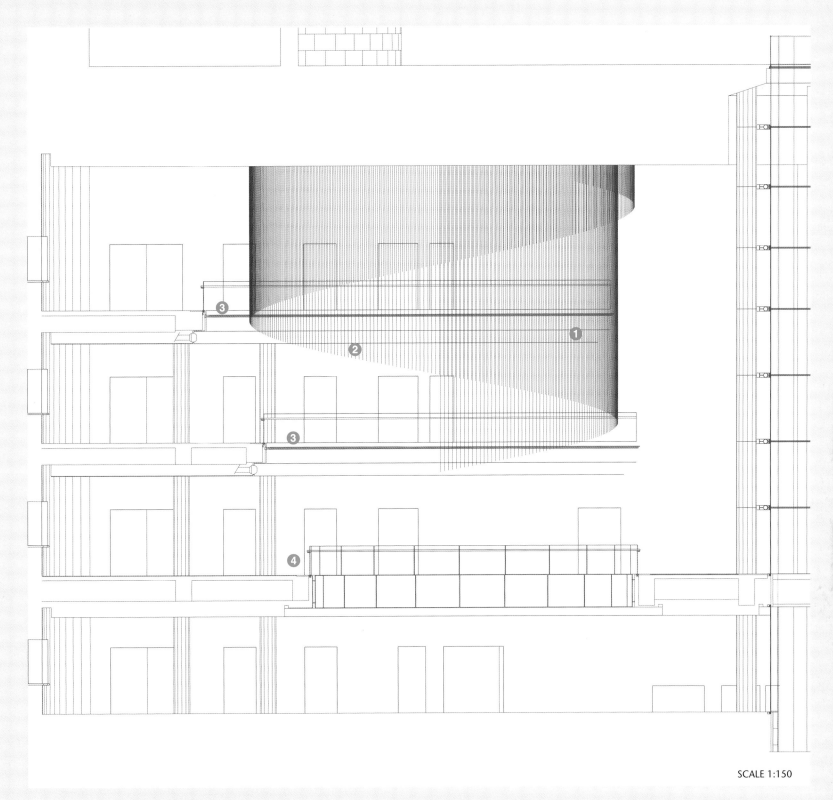

SCALE 1:150

ABOVE
Lobby elevation with chandelier
1 Stainless steel stems variable in length
from 45cm (18in) to llm (36ft)
2 Crystal diffuser on stainless steel housing
with 1W LED
3 Balcony fronts lit with white LEDs
4 Circle of honour, lit from ceiling-
recessed framing projectors

SHEIKH ZAYED BIN SULTAN AL NAHYAN MOSQUE, ABU DHABI
SPEIRS + MAJOR

One of the largest mosques in the world, this vast and intricately decorated building is designed to house more than 40,000 worshippers. It has 80 domes, including the main dome, the largest of its kind in the world at 70m (230ft) high and 30m (98ft) in diameter. Lighting it presented a series of creative and practical challenges, and often contradictory aims. The scheme had to provide coherence to the complex architecture and interior design while using an appropriate technique for each of a wide range of materials (marble panels, glass mosaic, carved gypsum, calligraphy). It also had to be sensitive to the architecture and atmosphere while remaining functional (including a strong lit image for normal, civic and TV events). The luminaires themselves (16,500 in all) had to be as discreetly located as possible.

The aim was to achieve as much of the light appearance and requisite levels using indirect wallwashing. Light sources were integrated into coves, niches, ledges and behind *musharabia* (carved wood latticework) details. The idea was that light should appear to be reflected, lending the space a luminosity. The main prayer hall, and in particular the *qibla* prayer wall – the 50m (164ft)-wide by 25m (82ft)-high structure towards which the worshippers face – was the key to the scheme. This involved a combination of techniques. The first is a wallwash from a 1,500mm (59in) cove, designed to illuminate the relief and marble finishes. The upper half is illuminated by 150W ceramic metal halide fittings with a wallwasher optic, while the lower portion is lit with 150W ceramic metal halide spots with a ribbed lens. Both fittings are set 2.5 degrees from the vertical, an optimum, factory-set position which resulted from a full-scale mock-up.

To illuminate the text (the 99 names, or qualities, of Allah), fibre optic channels create a fixed wash light to the internal gold mesh behind the cut-out calligraphy. Using a tight beam angle, the tilt was again factory set to light the face of the gold mesh correctly. Side-emitting fibre optics reveal the organic forms of vine-leaves and fronds. Niches at the base of the wall are lit with low-voltage tungsten halogen capsule lamps with a custom glass cover. These are dimmed to create a soft, diffused light to the niches and to balance the wallwashing from above.

RIGHT

The main prayer hall, the focal point of the building. The careful arrangement of lighting layers and details creates a composition with appropriate areas of emphasis and definition. Layers can be added or removed to respond to a variety of usages (here all lighting layers are on for a TV broadcast). The *qibla* wall is the focal point of the prayer hall and lit as a large 'gem-like' feature with integrated fibre optic lighting

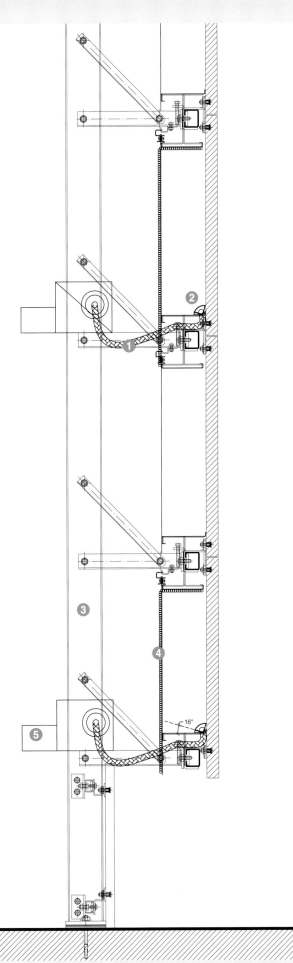

OPPOSITE

The *qibla* wall is lit using two fibre optic treatments. Side-emitting fibre optics are concealed in narrow recesses around the vine-like design so that the vines glow with a cool white light. The 99 names of Allah cut into the wall are backed by a gold curtain behind the face of the *qibla* wall. The names are lit using fibre optic channels focused on to the gold curtain, which is viewed through the inscriptions

LEFT

Detail showing the fibre optic channels lighting the inscriptions

1 Indicative fibre optic route
2 Fibre optic light channel attached to structural supports mounted on 16-degree shim plate
3 Maintenance ladder on slide rail
4 Gold curtain
5 Fibre optic lightbox

SCALE 1:12.5

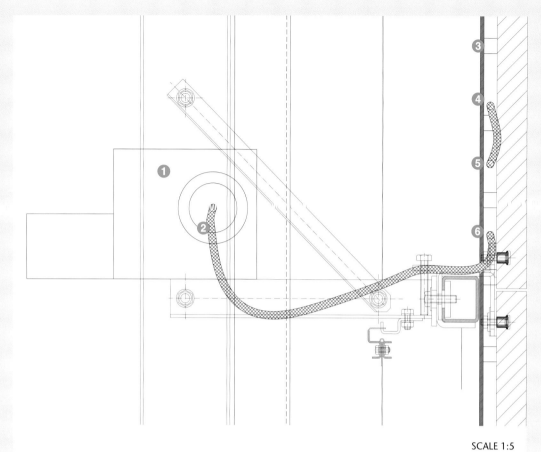

SCALE 1:5

LEFT

Section and plan details showing side-emitting fibre optics edge-lighting the vine pattern. It is carefully threaded through the internal construction of the wall and into the vines. The lightboxes for the fibre optics are accessible from the rear of the wall from catwalks for maintenance

1 Fibre optic illuminator mounted horizontally for optimum lamp performance

2 Threaded connection to fix fibre optic harness to illuminator

3 Wooden pegs at approximately 100mm (4in) intervals fixed to marble

4 5mm (1/sin) plywood board, finished matt white

5 Side cover to prevent light spill with intermediate fibre outlets fixed back to pegs

6 Side-emitting fibre optic cable

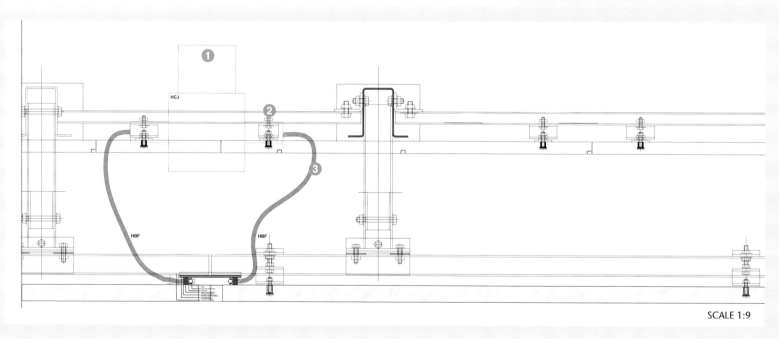

SCALE 1:9

ABOVE

1 Fibre optic lightbox mounted horizontally for optimum lamp performance

2 Threaded connection to fix fibre optic harness to lightbox

3 Bending radius minimized to 150mm (6in) to reduce damage to the fibre optic harness

LEFT
Lighting details were carefully integrated into both the physical and conceptual make-up of the wall. The effect is of a golden light emanating from beneath the surface

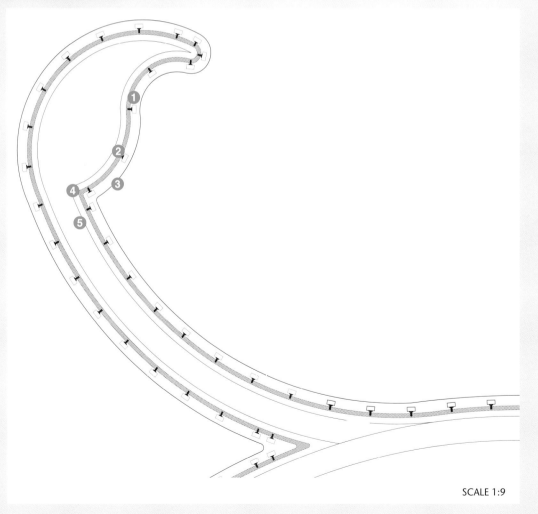

RIGHT
Internal elevation showing the side-emitting fibre optic detail for the vines. The fibre optic is set back out of sight around the vine and mounted to plasterboard panels, which close the vine opening. The effect is a subtle, continuous glow that tracks the line of the vine.
1 Wooden peg
2 C-clip
3 Plywood back-plate fixed to marble
4 Side-emitting fibre optic cable
5 Line of visible opening

SCALE 1:9

ZA-KOENJI PUBLIC THEATRE, TOKYO
LIGHTDESIGN INC.

Located in a Tokyo suburb, Toyo Ito's Za-Koenji Public Theatre is a conceptual metal structure designed to evoke the sense of a circus tent. The black steel skin covers a six-storey geometric structure, with three storeys below ground. The inspiration for the lighting is what is known in Japan as *komorebi* light, or sunshine filtering through foliage. This atmospheric play on light and shadow is created with a stylized use of circles, created using a variety of techniques.

As the sun shines from above through a leaf canopy, one lighting element is created by customized ceramic metal halide gobo projectors downlighting on to the floor in random patterns. A combination of 70W and 150W fixtures are used, both with cool white (4200K) lamps. Keeping the interior light levels very low allows these fittings to punch down powerfully into the space.

The theme is extended to the stairway where circular 8W compact fluorescent fittings with acrylic diffusers are integrated into the structure. Scattered round windows in the wall, which appear daylight blue, are also designed to suggest the brightness of sunlight viewed through foliage. Viewed from outside at night, these also allow the structure to glow with circles of light.

RIGHT
The concept is a stylized interpretation of *komorebi* light, or sunshine filtering through foliage. Circles of light are created using a variety of techniques

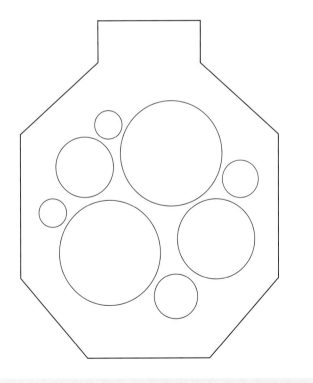

ABOVE
Floor patterning produced by ceramic metal halide gobo projectors

LEFT
Detail of gobo used on individual downlight projectors to create floor patterning

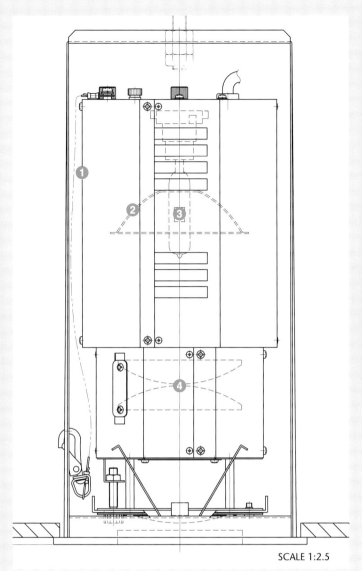

SCALE 1:2.5

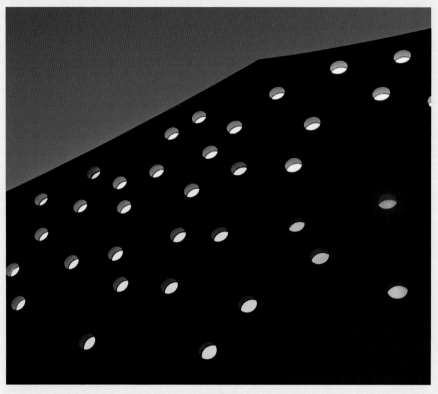

LEFT
Detail of 150W CDM-T downlight projector
1 Body steel, painted black
2 Reflector
3 Ceramic metal halide (CDM-T) lamp
4 Lens

ABOVE
Random round openings evoke *komorebi* light in the daytime interior space and create a striking effect for the night-time exterior

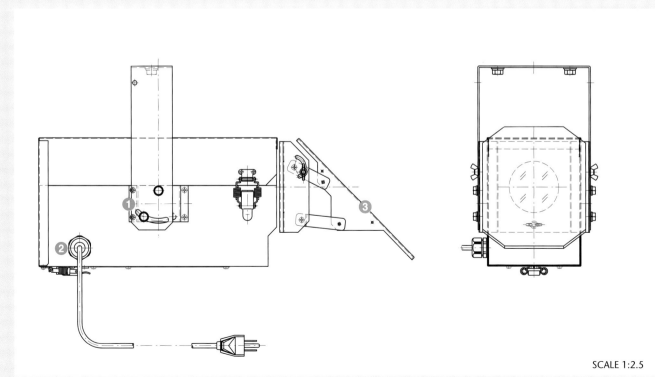

LEFT
Detail of 70W CDM-T spot projector
1 70W metal halide (4200K) lamp
2 Reflector
3 Stainless steel body, painted black to blend in with ceiling

SCALE 1:2.5

HOTELS & RESIDENCES

THE STUDIO, ANDAZ HOTEL, LONDON
ELEKTRA LIGHTING

The Studio is a next-generation hotel meeting room, which also functions as a private restaurant. The most striking feature in the space is the backlit Wovin Wall ceiling, the first time the material had been treated in this way. A bespoke fluorescent fitting allows light to spill through the spaces in the tiles, both enhancing the geometry of the ceiling and softening the lighting effect. Although the hotel's official policy is to have no fluorescent lighting in public areas, mock-ups proved that the source could produce an appropriate quality of illumination.

The special T5 fluorescent fitting with DSI dimming, developed with PJR Engineering, was carefully detailed to deal with the 195mm (7¾in) void. Both white and red light are used to create different moods according to the room's use, the mixing of the two allowing warm middle colours. Small 20W tungsten halogen uplights on wall columns soften the edges and there is also precise spotlighting on tables (through pre-drilled ceiling tiles). To cater for the changing uses of the space and also day/evening settings, an i-Light control system has 20 pre-programmed lighting scenes with an override for further flexibility.

RIGHT, TOP TO BOTTOM
The combination of red and white fluorescent light controlled by an iLight system creates warmer light for restaurant settings or cooler light when the space is used as a meeting room

OPPOSITE
Discreet spotlights, precisely mounted using pre-drilled holes in the tiles, allow pinspotting of tables for the restaurant mode

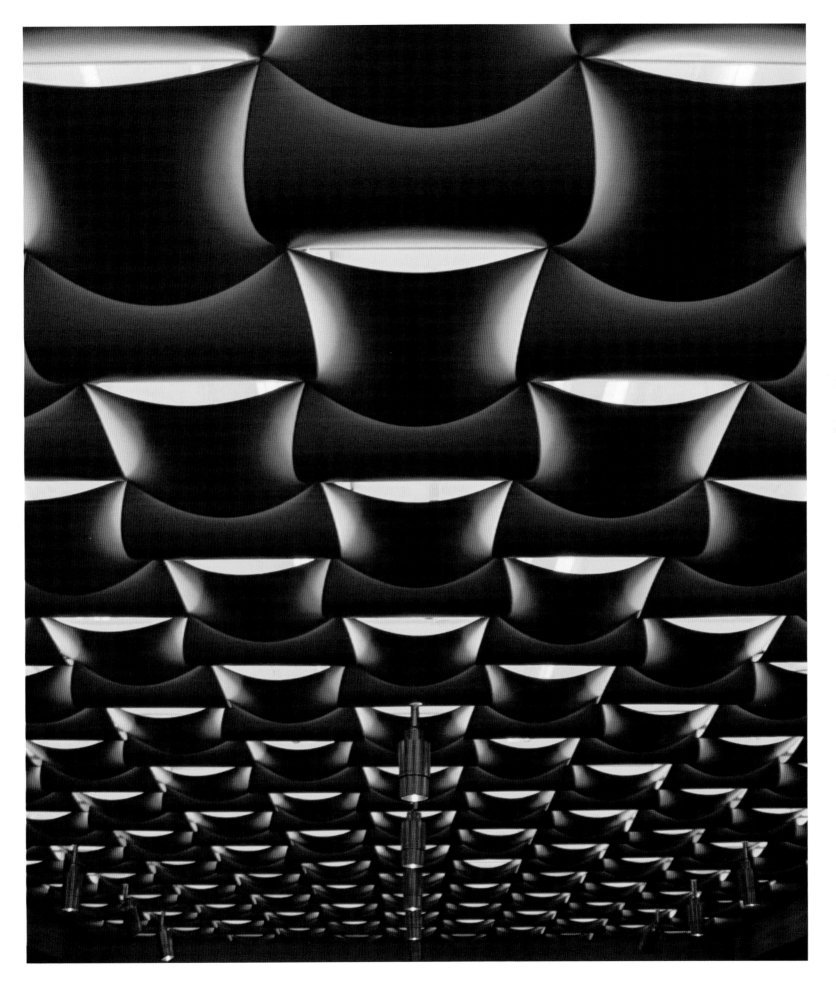

RIGHT
Plan view
1 Overlapping linear T5 fluorescent tubes
on custom tray. Each tray contains ten
dimmable lamps, five white and five
with red filter. Each colour is dimmed
separately with DSI control

OPPOSITE TOP
Section view
1 See detail below
2 Gear tray assembly on underside of
support beams
3 Tungsten halogen spotlights positioned
between fluorescent tubes

OPPOSITE BOTTOM
Detail of fluorescent fittings
4 White T5 lamp
5 T5 lamp with red filter
6 Dimmable ballasts, also mounted
on custom tray

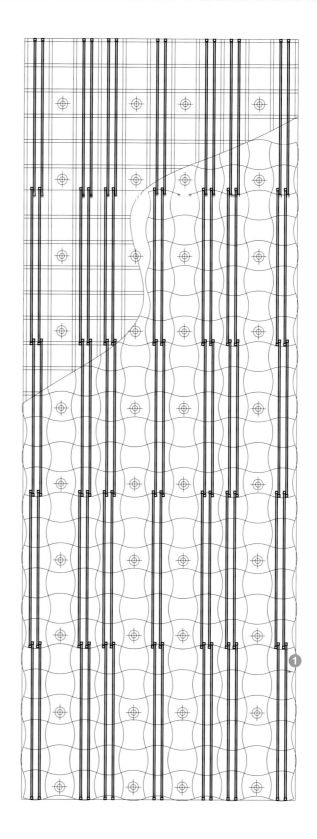

SCALE 1:50

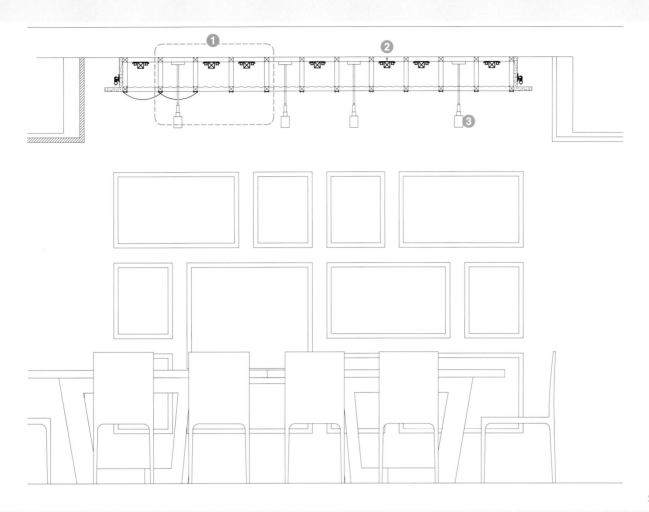

SCALE 1:25

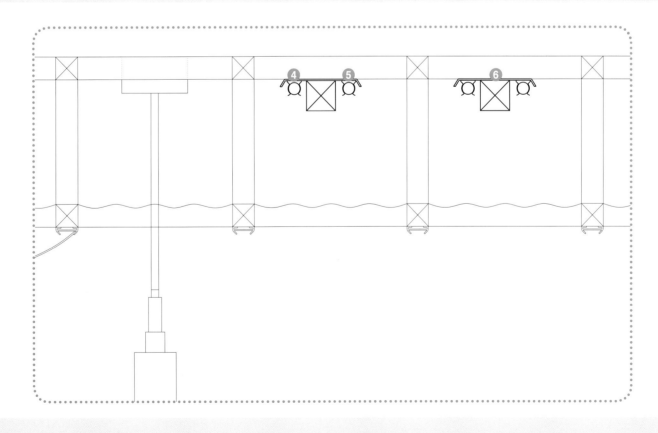

SCALE 1:5

CHAN RESTAURANT, THESSALONIKI
L+DG LIGHTING ARCHITECTS

Lighting is not only integrated into the interior of the Chan restaurant – a new Asian-inspired venue at the Met Hotel – but actually forms part of the architectural elements such as the metal wall and ceiling panels. Perforated in linear or concentric geometrical patterns these conceal cool white LEDs.

Several approaches to backlighting the panels were considered – the merits of integration compared with a stand-alone system, for instance, and of fibre optics versus LED strip-lighting – and all tested on a mock-up panel. The solution that was adopted involved the complete integration of LED striplighting into each panel, which was prefabricated complete with attached diffusing opalescent surface on the back. Wall panels measure 1m x 2.97m (3¼ft x 9¾ft), each using 86W. Ceiling panels vary in dimension and wattage but the two main sizes used are 2m x 1m (6½ft x 3¼ft) (58W per panel) and 1m x 0.7m (3¼ft x 2¼ft) (20W per panel).

The backlit perforated patterning is also picked up on the Corian bar, which is additionally highlighted with concealed LEDs.

In the restaurant area, additional localized lighting is provided by adjustable spotlights – MR16 or QR111 50W halogen lamps – concealed deep in special ceiling-recessed metallic drums that punctuate the ceiling panels. (Similar punctuations are used for other building services such as speakers and smoke detectors.) The same principle is used in the bar sitting area, this time with narrow-beam spotlights concealed above the horizontal fin structure of the false roof. Additional floor lamps provide accent lighting.

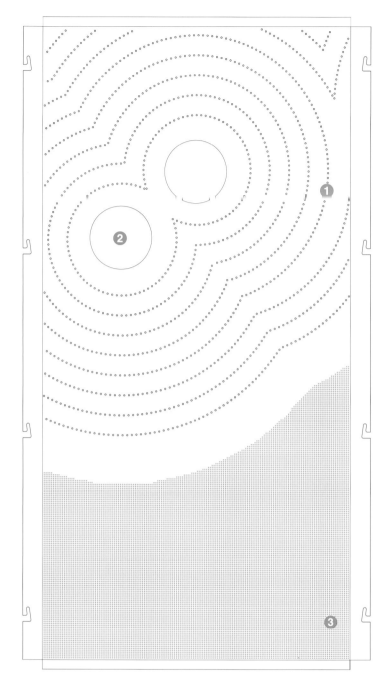

SCALE 1:12.5

ABOVE
Unfolded view of panel from above
1 Perforated holes (5mm/^{1}/$_5$in) backlit with cool white LEDs
2 Holes (200mm/7¾in diameter) for bespoke accent lighting and other services
3 Holes (2mm/^{1}/$_{12}$in diameter at 6mm/¼in centres) with black acoustic lining behind

OPPOSITE
Lighting and architectural elements are fused in the form of backlit perforated panels (restaurant area)

RIGHT

Reflected ceiling plan showing perforated ceiling panels (right) and integrated spotlighting.

1 Trimless fitting with recessed metal box integrating two deep-set adjustable spots with MR16 50W LV halogen lamp and remote transformers

2 Recessed directional fitting with one MR16 50W LV halogen lamp, deep set for glare control

3 Surface-mounted adjustable spot with AR111 50W LV halogen lamp and integrated transformer

4 Recessed trimless gimbal fitting with two adjustable AR111 50W LV halogen lamp and remote transformer

5 Trimless fitting with recessed metal box integrating two deep-set adjustable spots with MR16 50W LV halogen lamp and remote transformers

6 Linear LED system integrated in ceiling panels with remote power supply

7 Recessed fitting with one MR16 50W LV halogen lamp deep set for glare control, protective glass for IP44 and remote transformer

BOTTOM RIGHT

Detail of spotlighting in ceiling panel

1 Bespoke fitting with recessed metal box, black interior finish, integrating two deep-set adjustable spotlights housing low voltage MR16 (left) and ARIII (right) lamps with narrow-beam optics. Transformers are remote

2 Metal ceiling panel

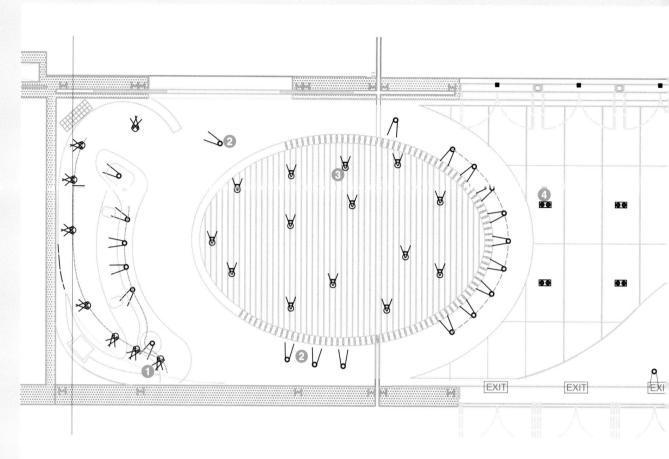

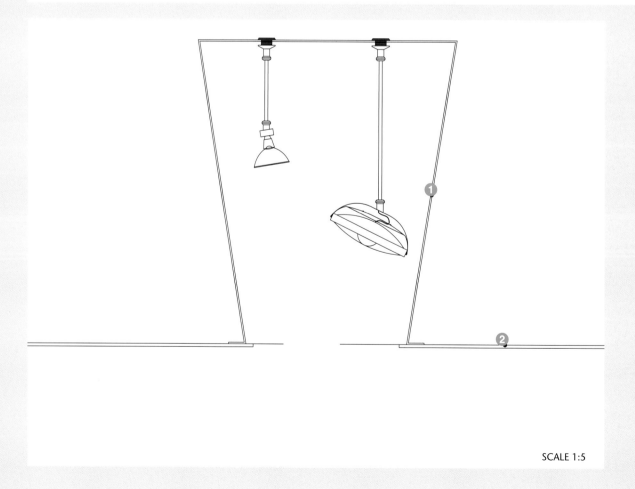

SCALE 1:5

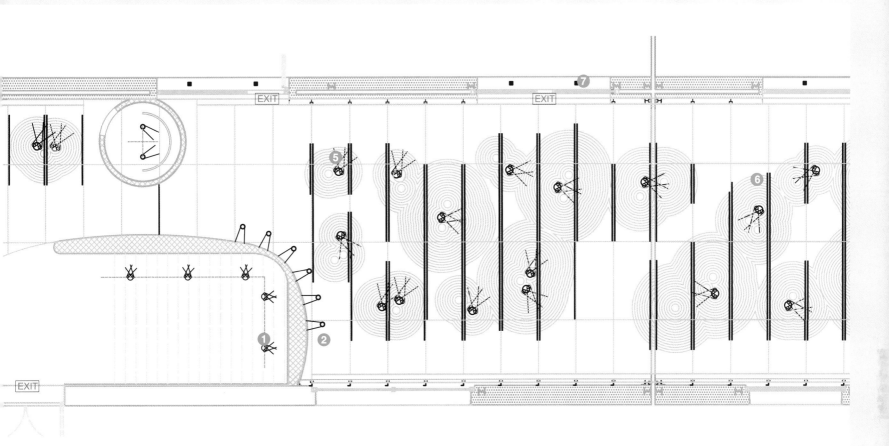

SCALE 1:100

LEFT
LED backlighting to the Corian bar echoes
the linear wall motif

ESPA AT THE EUROPE HOTEL, KILLARNEY, COUNTY KERRY
DPA LIGHTING CONSULTANTS

On the shores of Loch Lein in County Kerry, The Europe Hotel's setting was an inspiration for both interior and lighting design. A strong connection to nature, and specifically the loch itself, is an integral part of the lighting concept, which often plays on the relationship of light, reflection and shadow.

The partnership of light and water is used to dramatic effect in the Heat Experience Room. The wall of the vitality pool has integrated colour-changing LEDs. The interplay of this coloured light and the movement of the water creates a dynamic reflective lit pattern to the matt white ceiling above. The mood is reinforced with additional lighting elements such as fibre optic uplit wall niches.

A further lighting focal point is the ice fountain. To avoid the hazard of hot light fixtures on bare flesh, a fibre optic system is used to provide integrated illumination around the base. The remote projectors have 150W warm white (3000K) metal halide lamps, with the exception of the backlit ice, which has a cool 4200K lamp to represent the true colour of the ice bowl.

RIGHT
The interplay of light, water and shadow in the Heat Experience Room is fully exploited to create dynamic and dramatic effects

RIGHT

Section and plan views of ice fountain

1 Direction of lightbox

2 Recessed, flush narrow-beam fibre optic downlight (12 light points in total) with frosted cover illuminating solid glass rods and ice bowl. The lightbox, with warm white (3000K) 150W metal halide lamp, is located remotely in a dry, ventilated and accessible location

3 Recessed, flush-mounted wide-beam fibre optic uplight (12 light points in total) located in the base of ice bowl, with frosted cover to backlight ice. The lightbox, with cool white (4200K) I5OW metal halide lamp is located remotely in a dry, ventilated and accessible location

4 Recessed, inground, flush wide-beam fibre optic uplight (12 light points in total) with frosted cover uplighting the underside of the ice fountain. The light box, with warm white (3000K) 150W metal halide lamp, is located remotely in a dry, ventilated and accessible location

OPPOSITE TOP

Section (end view) of niche and pool lighting

1 Narrow-beam fibre optic spotlight recessed in bottom of niche

2 Recessed wide-beam RGB LED pool lighting with remote drivers positioned in a dry, ventilated and accessible location

3 Direction of lightbox

4 Direction of remote drivers

OPPOSITE BOTTOM

Section (side view) of niche and pool lighting

1 Fibre optic lightbox with 150W cool white (4200K) lamp, sited in a dry, ventilated and accessible location

2 Narrow-beam fibre optic spotlight recessed in bottom of niche

3 Recessed wide-beam RGB LED pool lighting with remote drivers positioned in a dry, ventilated and accessible location

4 Direction of remote drivers

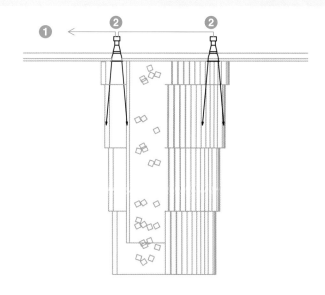

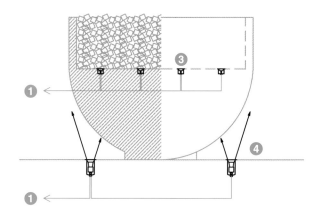

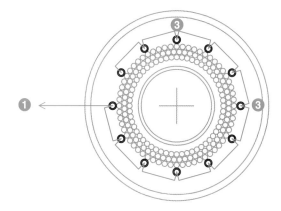

SCALE 1:25

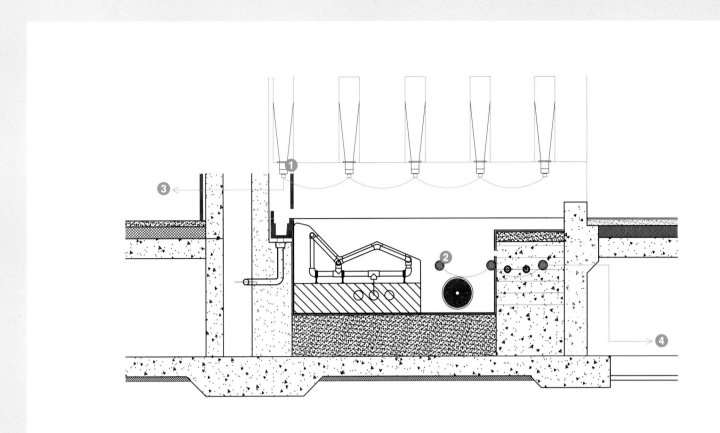

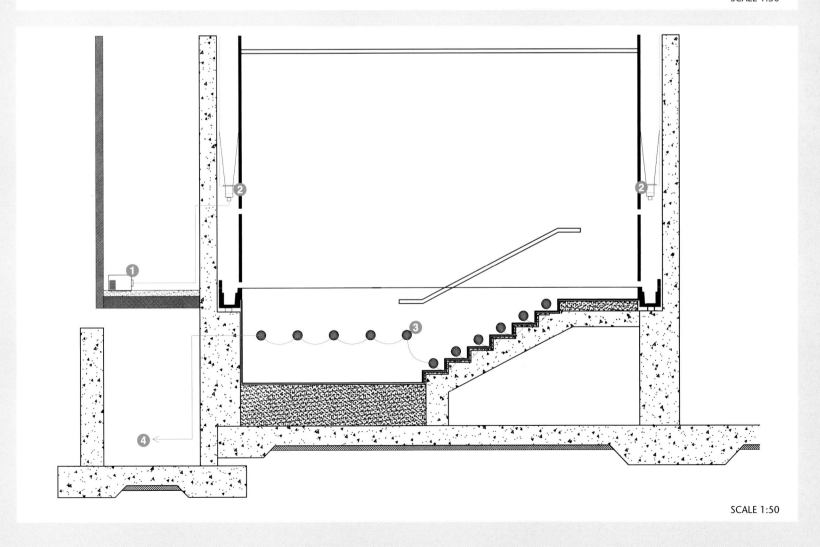

MANDARIN ORIENTAL HOTEL, BARCELONA
ISOMETRIX

Housed in a former 1930s bank building on Barcelona's iconic Passeig de Gracia, the Mandarin Oriental is designed to put contemporary luxury in a Catalan context. One of the main features of the hotel is its impressive entrance atrium, which is the core of the public areas.

The lighting strategy throughout was to avoid individual lighting elements such as downlights, spotlights and floor lamps. Instead the lighting is fully integrated into the architecture of each space in the form of lighting coves, linear details and concealed fixtures. This is exemplified in the atrium, both in the catwalk that bridges it and the illuminated window niches that rise up the wall to the large skylight at the top.

The catwalk rises up to the guest entrance, so that the carpet appears to lift off the floor, over the large atrium. Recessed linear slots with white cold cathode, which run parallel on either side, increase this sense of material definition between the carpet and the black gloss floor a number of metres below. The recessing of the lamp and the specification of the opal glass ensure that no lamp image or shadowing appear in the surface plate of the glass.

The niche effect is achieved in a similarly simple but very precise way. Warm white cold cathode (3000K) is positioned in the recesses sometimes above and sometimes to the side of the windows. An opal diffuser and matt white interior ensures a soft, even glow. The diffuser also controls the light so that it doesn't spill into the glazing. The lighting gradually dims according to the time of day, from 100 per cent to 15 per cent at night.

ABOVE
The niche lighting of the atrium windows typifies the integrated approach throughout the hotel

OPPOSITE
The recessed cold cathode on the rising catwalk increases the sense of material definition between the carpet and the black gloss floor metres below

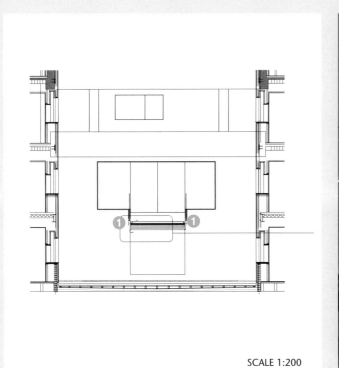

SCALE 1:200

ABOVE LEFT
Section of atrium catwalk
1 Recessed cold cathode either side
of catwalk

ABOVE
The recessed cold cathode on the rising
catwalk increases the sense of material
definition between the carpet and the
black gloss floor metres below

SCALE 1:10

ABOVE
Section detail of atrium catwalk
1 Ventilation gap
2 Special double layer of opal glass
(removable for maintenance)
3 Remote gear at accessible
ventilated location
4 Wet location-rated cold cathode

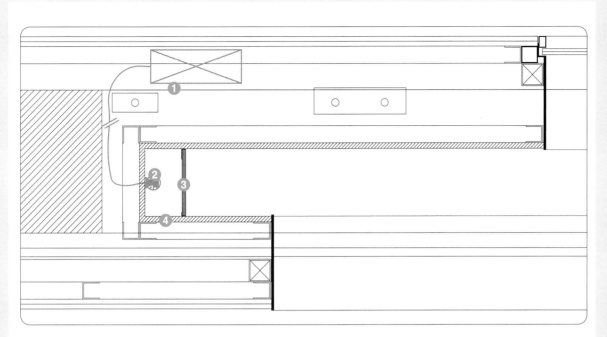

LEFT
Section detail of atrium window lighting
1 Remote gear at accessible
  ventilated location
2 Warm white cold cathode
3 Opal diffuser (removable
  for maintenance)
4 Matt white internal finish

SCALE 1:10

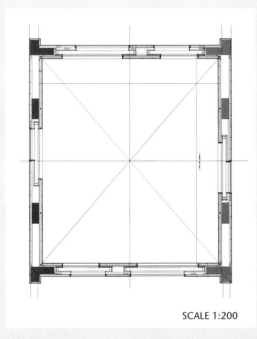

SCALE 1:200

ABOVE
Plan view of atrium window lighting

RIGHT
Illumination from the integrated cold
cathode is carefully controlled by an opal
diffuser to avoid light spill

THE MET HOTEL, THESSALONIKI
L+DG LIGHTING ARCHITECTS

The clean lines of this contemporary five-star urban hotel called for an integrated approach to the lighting. Although feature fittings such as the large pendants in the lobby are used judiciously to add drama, the primary lighting comes from a specially designed slot system. Used throughout, from bar to ballroom, the trimless profiles complement the geometry of the interior as well as providing a discreet housing for a variety of warm white (3000K) sources.

The slots have geometrical variations that relate to the particular space and house different kinds of spotlights, as well as cold cathode in some cases. This gives an aesthetic unity to all public areas throughout the hotel without sacrificing the specific lighting requirements for each space.

The general lighting for public areas and meeting rooms, for instance, is primarily MR16 and 75W QR111 low-voltage tungsten halogen lamps, both with anti-glare snoots, combined with dimmable low-voltage cold cathode for concealed linear lighting. Ceramic metal halide is added to the mix in the meeting room foyer and ballroom. All hotel corridors are lit with concealed low-voltage cold cathode plus MR16 accent lighting on guest-room doors.

The result is a harmonious and seamless lighting strategy that underlines architectural elements and creates the requisite drama.

RIGHT
The Long Bar: a specially designed slot system throughout allows a seamless, uniform approach that can nevertheless be tailored to specific spaces

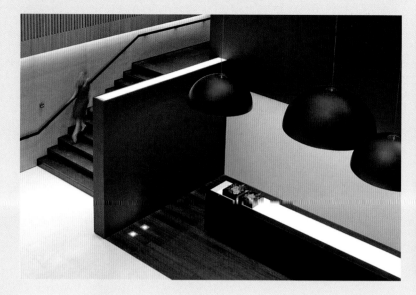

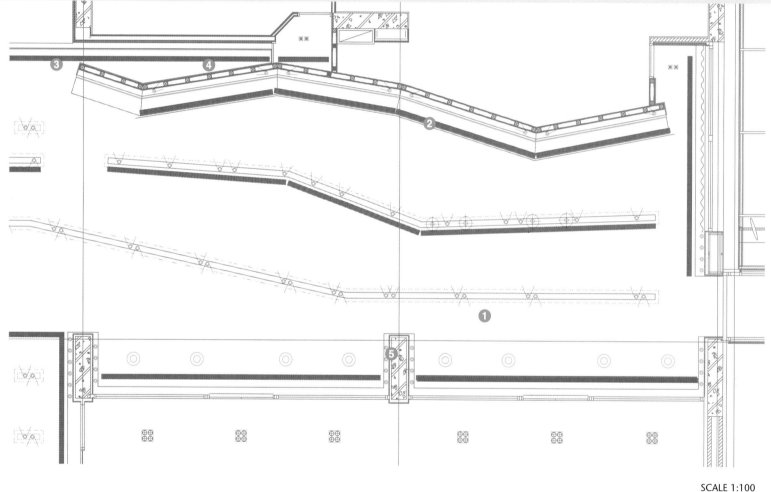

SCALE 1:100

TOP LEFT
Ballroom bar/foyer and grand staircase:
aside from occasional feature fittings,
lighting is linear and integrated
throughout to give an aesthetic unity

TOP RIGHT
In meeting rooms, linear ceiling and wall
slots have integrated cold cathode for a
luminous effect and general lighting. Wall
fittings and pendants add a further layer

ABOVE
RCP of the Long Bar
(pictured previous page)
1 Housed in black-painted slot, adjustable LV
halogen spotlights with reflector exterior
painted black to eliminate backlighting
2 Housed in white-painted slot, adjustable
recessed spotlight with narrow-beam
MR16 lamp and warm white cold
cathode tube

3 Housed in white-painted slot, warm
white cold cathode tube for illuminated
ceiling slot
4 Housed in white-painted slot along
wall, warm white cold cathode tube for
wallwashing.
5 Housed in black-painted slot, deep-
set halogen lamp spotlight for accent
lighting on rectangular columns

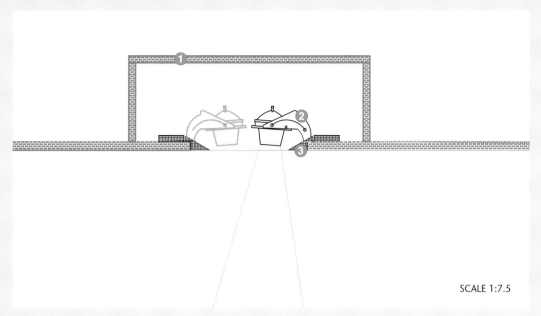

SCALE 1:7.5

LEFT
Detail of slot system in lobby
1 Gypsum board boxing painted black internally
2 Special adjustable LV spotlight housing MR16 lamp with reflector painted black on the outside to eliminate backlighting, anti-glare snoot and remote transformer
3 Special aluminium profile attached to gypsum board ceiling to create trimless edge. Spots are installed on profile

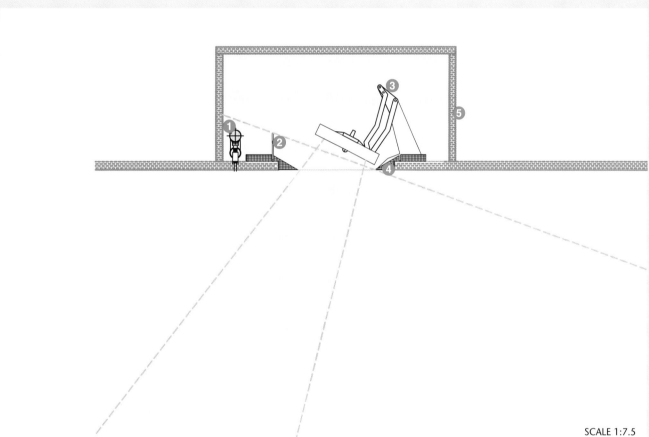

SCALE 1:7.5

ABOVE
Detail of slot system in foyer
1 Low-voltage cold cathode to illuminate ceiling slot
2 Diffusing glass to conceal cold cathode
3 Adjustable spotlights with ARIII LV halogen or metal halide lamp with medium beam reflector
4 Special aluminium profile attached to gypsum board ceiling to create trimless edge. Spots are installed on profile
5 Gypsum board boxing painted white internally

OPPOSITE HOUSE HOTEL, BEIJING
ISOMETRIX

The Opposite House, an international brand of five-star hotel, is in the centre of Sanlitun Village, a new retail, arts and leisure development in Beijing's diplomatic quarter. The architectural concept was to take traditional forms of material and spaces found in old Beijing workshops and townhouses, and reinterpret them using cutting-edge construction techniques. The building is oriented around a series of courtyards or voids open to sky light in some places.

All ambient lighting is limited to either floor or ceiling slots and whatever the lamp – LEDs, fluorescent, cold cathode, halogen – the colour temperature is a warm 3000K throughout. This not only provides cross uniformity but allows the different materials – traditional wooden fabric screens, steel, concrete and glass – to stand out in greater contrast.

Each void was given a distinct look. In the case of the double-height swimming pool, 1mm ($^{1}/_{25}$in) fibre optic tails are suspended from the ceiling and dropped the full building height to the pool in the basement, creating a three-dimensional sculpture of floating light points that fill the space and lead the eye down to the water. The pendants form a single plane above the water. Each single fibre terminates in a pendant downlight that keeps the fibre taut. The fibre is slightly crushed along its length to give it a subtle presence. All fibre optic illuminators use 150W ceramic metal halide lamps (CRI85).

At the base of the pool are two rows of side-emitting fibre optic cables skimming light across the pool bottom. This also forms a very defined plane as it maximizes the diffraction properties of the water. The glass walls are backlit with two rows of warm white T5 fluorescent lamps, carefully diffused, deep recessed within the floor, washing up to a white painted wall behind the frosted glass. The rear wall is a straightforward ceiling cove to a solid wall using a single row of warm white cold cathode. The light reflected in the surface of the water and wall material creates dramatic infinity effects and plays with the dimensions of the space.

RIGHT
The fibre optic pendants create a secondary ceiling plane that floats elegantly above the pool to form a single plane above the water

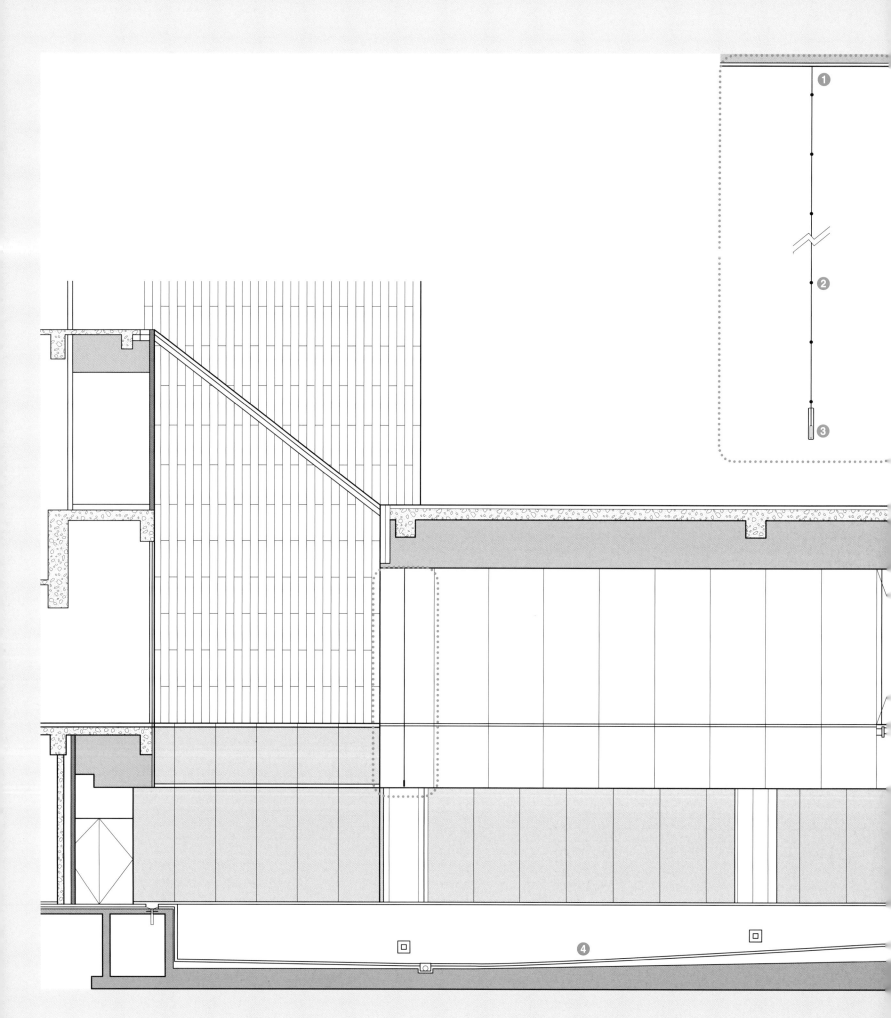

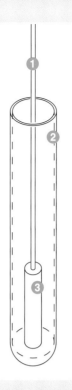

FAR LEFT

1 1mm ($^{1}/_{2}$sin) fibre optic strand suspended from ceiling

2 Distress points by controlled laser exposure

3 Bottom tube and stopper

4 Side-emitting fibre cable at bottom of pool

LEFT

Detail of individual fibre optic light point

1 1mm ($^{1}/_{2}$sin) fibre optic tail

2 Clear acrylic tube, 100mm (4in) height, 5mm ($^{1}/_{8}$in) diameter

3 Bottom stopper, frosted plastic

BELOW

Fibre optics tails are suspended from the double-height ceiling to create a three-dimensional sculpture of floating light points

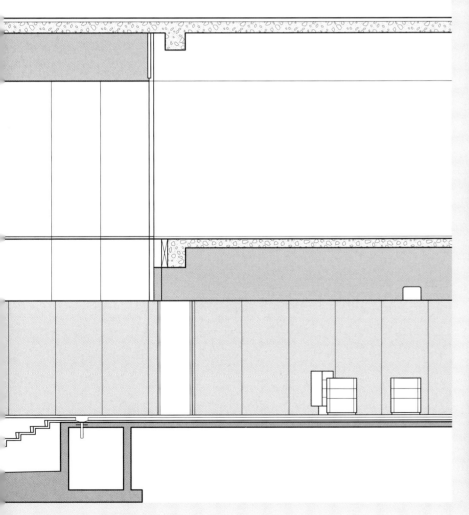

PRIVATE RESIDENCE, MISSOURI
DEREK PORTER STUDIO

This single-storey residence is clad in full-height perforated COR-TEN steel panels, which envelop the entire exterior apart from intervals for glazing. The idea of 'skin and particle' – the outer shroud containing internal activity ('particle') – is central to the lighting design. The wash of light at the perimeter is complemented by scattered patterns of small scale recessed accent lights inside. While the illuminance varies, the colour temperature and rendering are consistent so they blend homogeneously.

To create the lighting 'skin', a custom outdoor luminaire was developed to fit between the external metal panels and the rain screen all around the house. These fixtures light the immediate landscape, but also provide interior illumination at select areas, eroding the sense of separation between the built environment and nature.

The 1,054mm (41½in)-long luminaires are mounted at the top of the interstitial space, within the brackets of the panels that cantilever from the building's structural columns. The lamps are warm white (3000K) 14W standard output T5 fluorescent tubes, overlapping to create an even illumination. A minimum angle of rotation allows access underneath for ballast and lamp maintenance (done from above, without the need to remove the steel panels).

For exterior illumination, the light first reflects off the rear of the perforated panel, then off the white rain screen and projects through the perforated holes, bouncing and reflecting inside the cavity. This produces a soft gradation of light (brighter at the top) as the light moves downwards, blurring boundaries between interior and exterior.

Where there is a full-height window, the perforated panel becomes a short skirt at the top of the glazing. Here the light is oriented towards the rear of the perforated metal panel and reflects into the interior. From inside looking out, only the illuminated side of the panel is visible – the house side of the luminaire has a longer 'visual' shield to reduce the likelihood of seeing the fittings from normal viewing angles – whereas from the exterior the panel is always seen in shadow, or silhouette. Again this differentiation is intentional, reinforcing the skin metaphor.

RIGHT AND OPPOSITE
The light fittings sit between perforated metal panels and the rain screen all around the top of the house, gently washing the exterior and reflecting into the interior above the glazing

SCALE 1:300

ABOVE

Plan view of house

1 Perforated COR-TEN steel panels
enveloping exterior walls

2 Glazing

3 T5 fluorescent fittings at top between
steel panels and rain wall

4 Scattered patterns of recessed accent
lighting representing the 'particle' part
of the concept

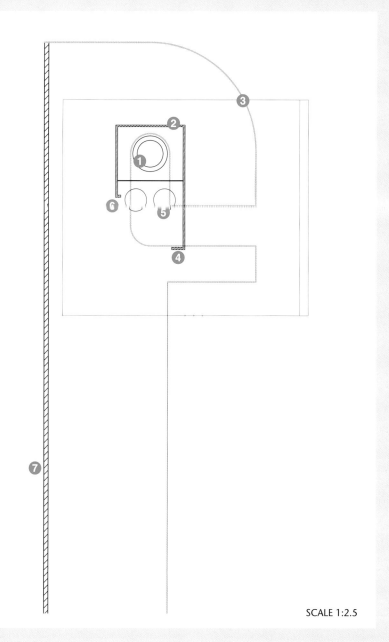

SCALE 1:2.5

ABOVE

Section of luminaire

1 2.5cm (1in) pipe supporting
metal panels

2 Custom sheet-metal shield

3 Metal perforated panel clip

4 Longer shield on house side to reduce
likelihood of seeing the light from
normal viewing angles

5 Single overlapping T5 fluorescent lamp

6 Extended skirt preventing water from
touching electrical components

7 Steel panel

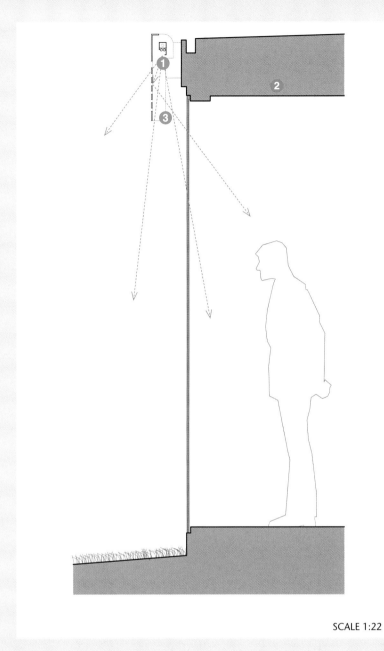

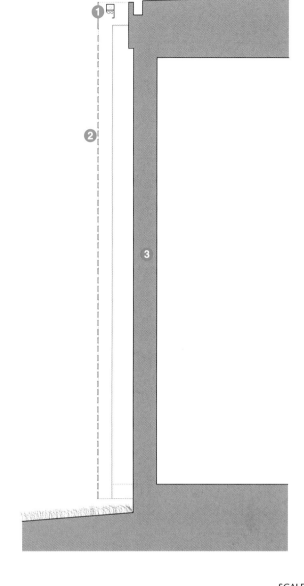

SCALE 1:22

SCALE 1:22

ABOVE

Section of wall showing light distribution

1 Single overlapping T5 fluorescent lamp

2 Dark ceiling in interior

3 The illuminated side of the perforated
   panel, which is viewed from the interior

ABOVE

Section of wall

1 Single overlapping T5 fluorescent lamp

2 Perforated Cor-ten steel panel
   (full height)

3 Rain screen (full height), white to
   maximize reflectance the entire length
   of the cavity

PRIVATE RESIDENTIAL SPA, LOCATION UNDISCLOSED
LIGHTING DESIGN INTERNATIONAL

This residential spa was created in a newly carved-out basement. The brief was to create a series of calm and coherent spaces where the lighting both complemented, and was integral to, the architecture. The aim was to see the light effect not the source, and the challenge in such a stark space was to hide all visible technology, concealing it with clever coordination and custom detailing. The pool is internally clad with Black Sicilian Basaltina, which mirrors the play of light across the undulating GRG (glass-reinforced gypsum) ceiling above. A skylight lights the end wall naturally by day (balanced by artificial light at night), reflecting light across the space and accentuating the ceiling's sculptural form. The ceiling of the pool is halo-lit from its angular perimeter. Two concealed indirect light sources – cold cathode and LEDs – bounce light down the walls, defining the structure's peaks and troughs with a dramatic line of light. The cold cathode lights the space by day in a crisp mid-white (3500K), while colour-changing LEDs provide a warm white glow or selected colours during the evening. The trough provides almost all of the high-level illumination, with no lighting allowed to penetrate the ceiling. The pool itself is lit from two sides by banks of narrow-beam, cool white LEDs. The scheme delineates the space, exploring simple relationships between stone, water and light.

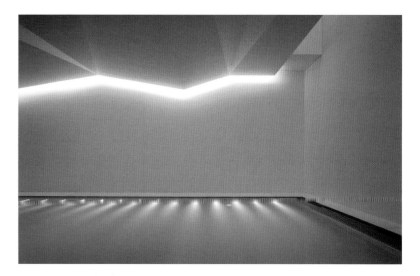

TOP RIGHT
Concealed 3500K mid-white cold cathode defines the ceiling form, balanced by daylight to the end wall, while narrow-beam LEDs provide dramatic underwater lighting

ABOVE RIGHT
Colour-variable LEDs create a warm, saturated glow during the evening or pre-selected colours. Underwater lighting is switched off for striking reflections and a more subdued mood

RIGHT
Interior finishes in the steam room are darker, with corner-recessed mood lighting defining the boundaries and framing the view of the pool

OPPOSITE
The perimeter trough conceals all fittings and provides almost all of the high-level illumination, with no lighting allowed to penetrate the ceiling

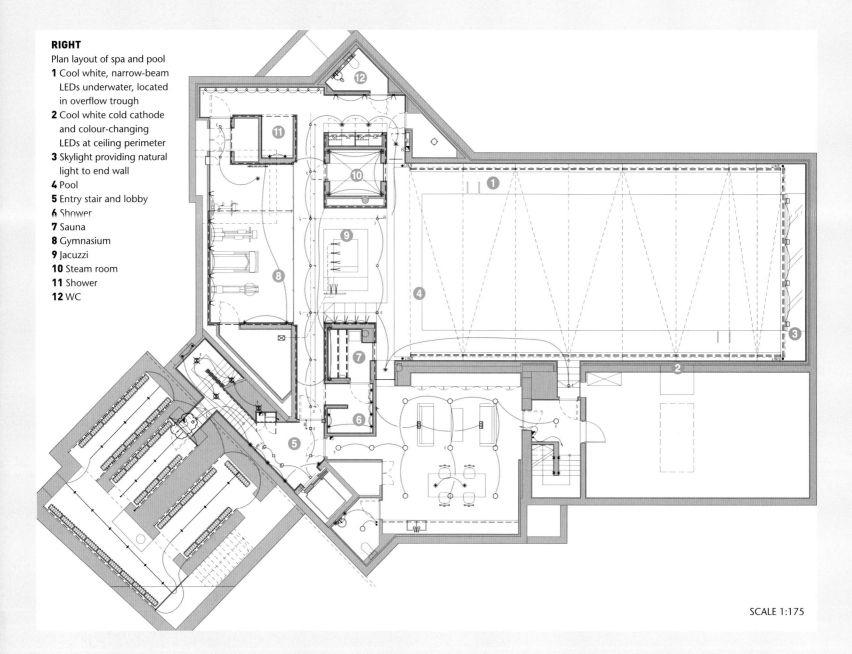

RIGHT

Plan layout of spa and pool

1 Cool white, narrow-beam LEDs underwater, located in overflow trough

2 Cool white cold cathode and colour-changing LEDs at ceiling perimeter

3 Skylight providing natural light to end wall

4 Pool

5 Entry stair and lobby

6 Shower

7 Sauna

8 Gymnasium

9 Jacuzzi

10 Steam room

11 Shower

12 WC

SCALE 1:175

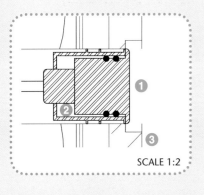

SCALE 1:2

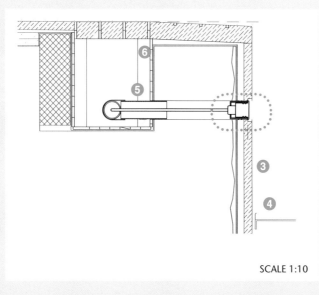

SCALE 1:10

LEFT

Narrow-beam, cool white LEDs provide underwater lighting from either side of the pool. This solution was implemented after a raise-and-lower pool floor was introduced, which would have covered the original pool floodlights. The pool was already cast prior to LDI's involvement, so these fittings were installed 200mm (8in) below the water's surface. This meant that cabling and maintenance could be achieved through the pool's overflow channel with specialist detailing

1 Narrow-beam LED fitting

2 LED housing sealed into stone

3 Stone pool interior

4 Raise-and-lower pool floor

5 Sealed cabling route

6 Pool overflow channel

BELOW
[section through high point]

The indirect ceiling slot detail that provides the halo-lighting conceals cold cathode with turned-back electrodes, linear colour-variable LED fittings and AC slots. All lighting is mounted neatly to lift-out wooden templates to aid installation, positioning and maintenance. LEDs are angled to skim over the cold cathode tubes, minimizing visible shadows, and all cabling is also fixed down for the same reason

1 Linear colour-change LED profile
2 3500K white cold cathode
3 Drivers and control gear

RIGHT
[section through low point]

The ceiling was produced in large sections off-site from GRG, which was then pieced together and hung from the concrete slab. As the accuracy and buildability of such a complex form was a concern, the lighting trough detail and internal trough ceiling was cast as part of the main GRG structure to ensure a seamless harmony. A 10mm (⅖in) shadow gap was also introduced at the edge of the GRG to differentiate this material from the limestone wall it would be butting against. The cast ceiling conceals a network of tapering air ducts, acting like a huge plenum that provides the environmental controls for the pool area with the lighting channel following the same profile

1 Linear LED lighting
2 Single run of 20mm (7¾in) cold cathode
3 Drivers and control gear
4 Internal ceiling
5 AC Duct
6 AC Grill

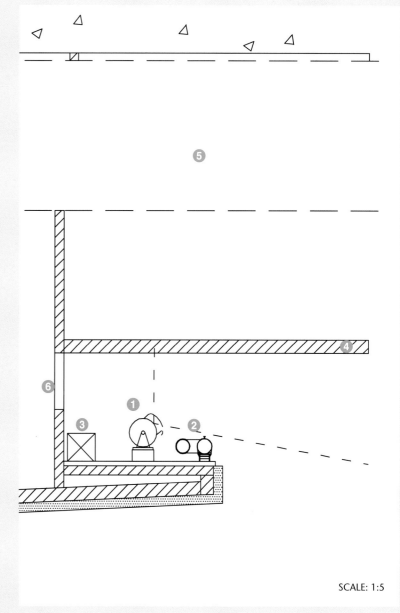

SCALE: 1:5

SCALE: 1:6

RIGHT
[section 03]

Cold cathode lamps were custom made to match the lengths of the faceted ceiling, with turned-back electrodes, allowing the tubes to be illuminated all the way to their ends and eliminating shadows between lamps

1 Linear colour-change LED profile
2 3500K white cold cathode

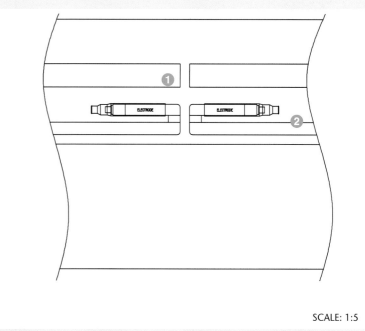

SCALE: 1:5

THE ROTUNDA, BIRMINGHAM
MINDSEYE LIGHTING

Originally a 25-storey office block, the Rotunda has been a landmark in the centre of the UK city of Birmingham since the 1960s. The Grade II-listed cylindrical building has recently been refurbished – part of the massive redevelopment of the second city's iconic Bullring Centre – and converted into 232 residential apartments. The lighting brief was for a dramatic feature which would fill a 9m (29½ft) void in the upgraded entrance lobby.

The installation, effectively a giant chandelier, comprises 437 custom-manufactured polished aluminium tubes with colour-changing LEDs at the end of each one. Measuring 14.5m (47½ft) long and 4.8m (15¾ft) at the widest point, the 46 rows of tubes running front to back are attached directly to the ceiling and form a wave shape. The contour and layout were designed to maximize interest and viewing angles for the public. The highest tubes are 6m (19½ft) from the ground while the longest tubes drop 6m (19½ft), with a total of 940m (3,083ft) of tube used to achieve the desired effect. At the end of each tube is a 45mm (1¾in)-diameter VersaPIXEL 1W RGB LED fitting, each individually addressable to create dynamic colour effects.

The ceiling has a calculated weight loading to enable the tubes to be fixed directly to it using bayonet-type aluminium internal tube fixing brackets with custom spring safety clips. An important stipulation was that the tubes should seem to disappear into the ceiling – no access hatches were permitted anywhere in the atrium for control equipment and no fixings or bracketry could be visible. Ahead of the ceiling installation, the cables were pre-hung and labelled in the roof before being pulled through and plastered around once the ceiling was in place.

The three Element Labs' PSUBBs and 16 P-HUB32s signal distributors had to be located in special external access hatches. This in turn meant that 437 custom 9m (29½ft) cables also had to be created for each of the pixels, allowing the tubes to be individually removed from the bottom for easy maintenance.

The LEDs are controlled from behind the reception desk using an eight-button user interface, a Pharos LPC-1 and an Element Labs VersaDRIVE C1. Eight custom video clips were created providing eight different lighting scenes. The content clips loop every five minutes, providing continuous waves of colour. As the content is predominantly coloured, although the installed load is more than 400W, the actual energy consumption is around 200W.

ABOVE AND OPPOSITE
More than 400 custom-made aluminium tubes, each with a colour-changing LED, form a giant chandelier that fills a 9m (29½ft) void in the redeveloped Rotunda's entrance lobby

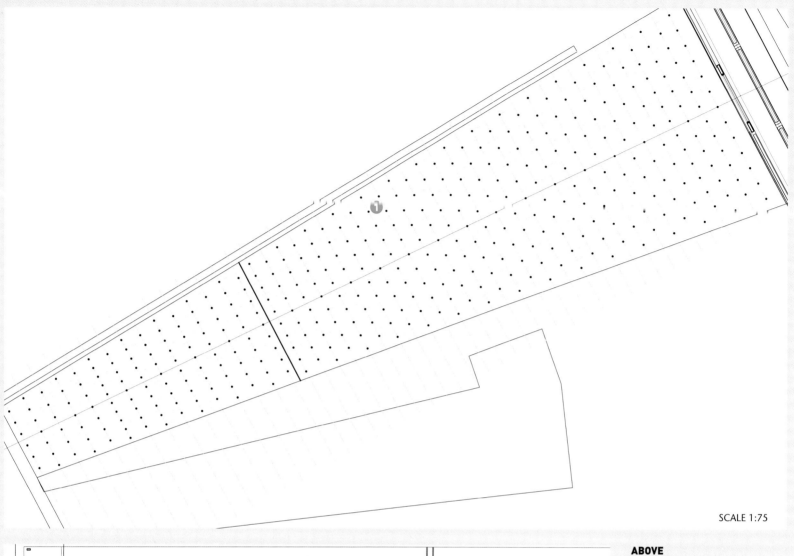

SCALE 1:75

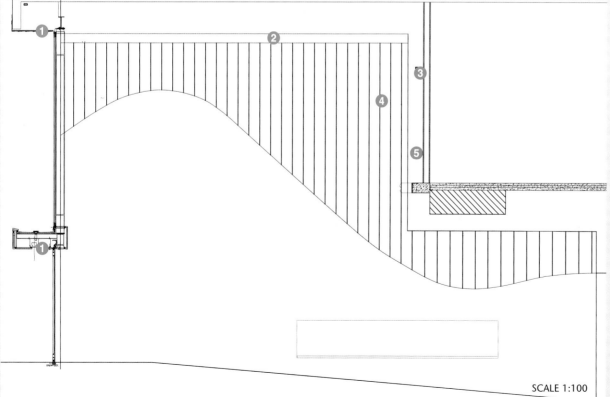

SCALE 1:100

ABOVE
Plan view of the composition
of tubes
1 Individual tubes with 1W RGB
LED fitting

LEFT
Curve section
1 P-HUB 32 signal distributors
to cover front section of LEDs
(approx. five P-HUB32s per
152 pixels)
2 Ceiling has calculated weight
loading allowing tubes to be fixed
directly to it
3 P-HUB 32 signal distributors
to cover middle section of LEDs
(approx. five P-HUB32s per
143 pixels)
4 Polished aluminium tubes, the
highest 6m (19½ft) from the
ground and the longest dropping
6m (19½ft) to form a wave shape
5 P-HUB 32 signal distributors
to cover rear section of LEDs
(approx. five P-HUB32s per
142 pixels)

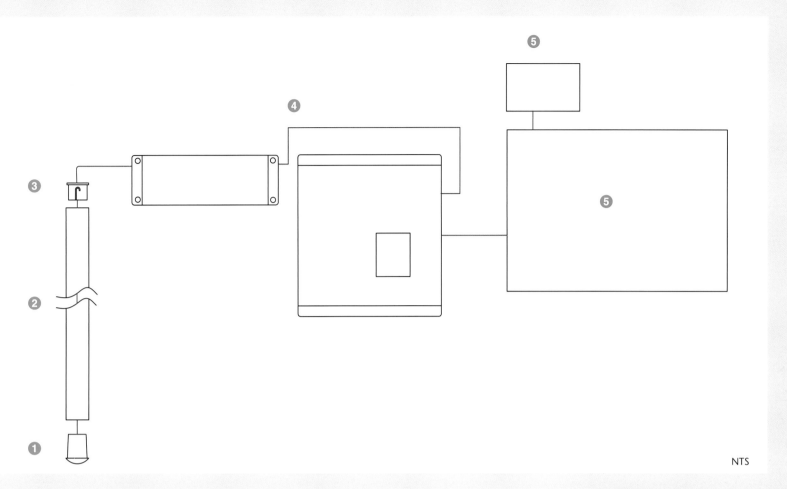

NTS

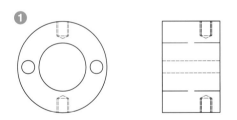

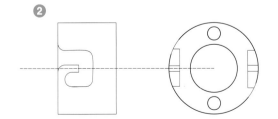

ABOVE
Plan view of the composition
of tubes
1 LED pixel
2 Tube
3 Surface fixing
4 LED transformer
5 Control equipment (x2)

LEFT
Mounting arrangement for tubes
1 Screw fixed (removable only from
the surface fixing at ceiling level).
Screw-fix concept allows the tubes
to be securely fixed, especially for
the lower height areas.
2 The J-slot allows the tube to
be released from the LED end,
making it easy for maintenance.
Detail of the J-slot is closely coordinated with the position of the
bolts within the aluminium tubes.

SCALE 1:1.5

137

RUENTEX TUNHUA-RENAI CONDOMINIUM, TAIPEI
CMA LIGHTING DESIGN

The 27-storey Ruentex Tunhua-Renai condominium is located in one of Taipei's most prestigious districts. The entrance to the residential part of the building makes a striking statement: a three-dimensional egg-shaped lobby, formed from a steel pipe structure covered with woven wooden slats. During the day sunlight shines through this screen, creating woven patterns in the interior. The aim with the artificial lighting was to recreate this atmosphere – soft lighting with a degree of shadow – but to reverse the concept by allowing the lobby to act as a lantern.

Part of this effect is achieved with continuous LED lighting (low-energy sources were also a key stipulation). The 63cm (25in) 'belt lights' (1W 3000K LEDs at a beam angle of 120 degrees) sit in a curved channel under frosted rib glass at the base of the egg. Par 30-type 12W LED fittings hung from the ceiling increase the ambient illumination, supplemented by free-standing luminaires, but an even lighting effect was avoided in line with the overall aim of contrast.

However the architect also wanted a surreal lighting element. A customized fitting dubbed the 'cigar light' is the key fitting within the space, both defining the unusual egg form and acting as a stylistic device. A 25cm (10in)-diameter steel plate sits at each joint of the structure on which is mounted the 20cm (8in)-long acrylic tube, partially sandblasted to produce a satin effect. A 3000K 1W LED is concealed in the metal base. More than 150 are used in all, with half pointed inwards, the other half outwards.

ABOVE, TOP AND BOTTOM
The entrance to the egg-shaped lobby viewed from the front and the side

OPPOSITE
The key fitting inside the lobby is the specially designed 'cigar' light, which acts as a decorative element while also delineating the ovoid shape. The LED belt light defines the base of the structure

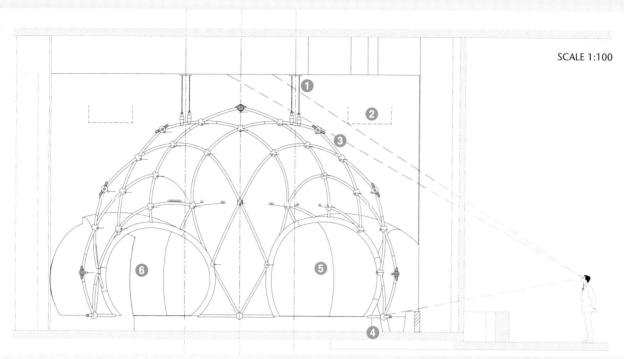

LEFT
Section of lobby
1 Downlights
2 Catwalk
3 Cigar light
4 LED belt light
5 Counter
6 Mailbox

BELOW
Floor plan of lobby
1 Continuous LED
illumination from floor-
recessed belt fittings
2 Reception

SCALE 1:100

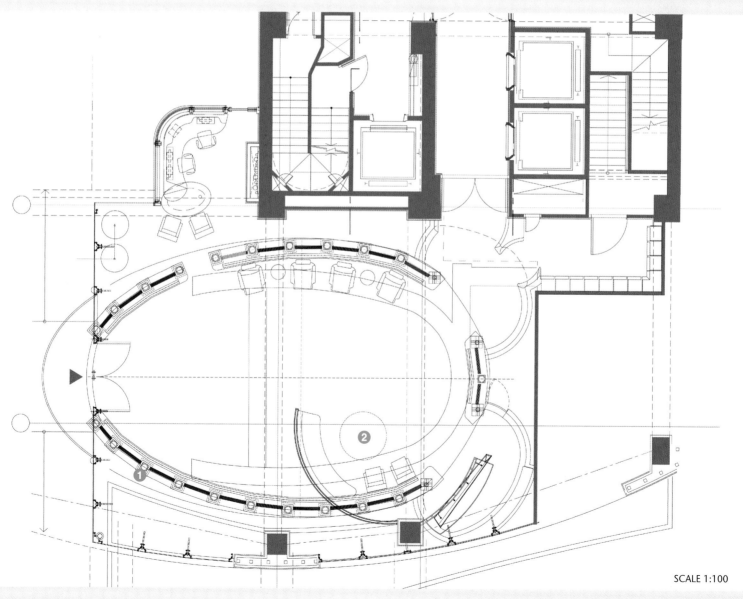

SCALE 1:100

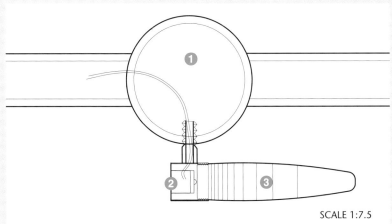

LEFT
Section detail of cigar light
1 25cm (10in)-diameter metal plate
2 1W LED
3 20cm (8in) sandblasted acrylic rod
with the 4cm (1½in) tip left clear

SCALE 1:7.5

ABOVE
The 20cm (8in)-long acrylic cigar light is
partially sandblasted to produce a satin
effect. The metal base houses a 3000K
1W LED

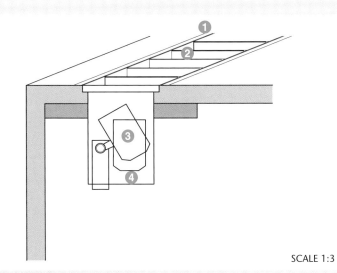

LEFT
Section of 'belt lights', which provide
continuous lighting at the base of the egg
1 Metal louvre cover
2 Metal screen
3 1W 3000K LED spotlight with beam
angle of 120 degrees
4 Metal housing

SCALE 1:3

SOUND NIGHTCLUB, PHUKET
INVERSE LIGHTING DESIGN

The fusion of music, light and space was the main concept for the Sound Club. The lighting is integral to interior elements, tracing their sinuous lines and organic forms, while also directly responding to the changing rhythm and pitch of the music. That response in turn affects perception of the space. Central to this effect are the pod seating areas and the corridor which leads to the main dance floor.

The seating pods have blue LEDs along the base, which create a floating effect. Flexible LED striplighting outlines the curved steps and the continuous blue LEDs positioned underneath the pods reveal the form of the seats. Blue LEDs also lend a subtle glow to the acrylic screen at the top which outlines the 'ear' shape of the seating. A narrow-beam, 2W LED spot fitted with a custom snoot provides accent light to the table. The pod lighting is linked to the music: the low level lights respond to bass notes, while the glowing lights at the top respond to high tones.

The corridor is a tunnel-like space with concealed lighting in vertical slots along its length. As people walk towards the dance floor, the changing intensity and movement of light creates the impression that the walls are animated: the space appears to breathe with the sound wave coming towards them. This is achieved with individually addressable 70mm (2¾in) sections of blue LEDs, each of which acts like a pixel. Controlling the effect are around 1,500 channels linked to three DMX512 universes (networks). Different effects have been programmed but the system can also be manually adjusted, allowing the LJ and VJ greater flexibility.

RIGHT
The dance floor with its organic shaped seating pods. The concealed lighting at the top and bottom of the pods responds to the rhythm and pitch of the music.

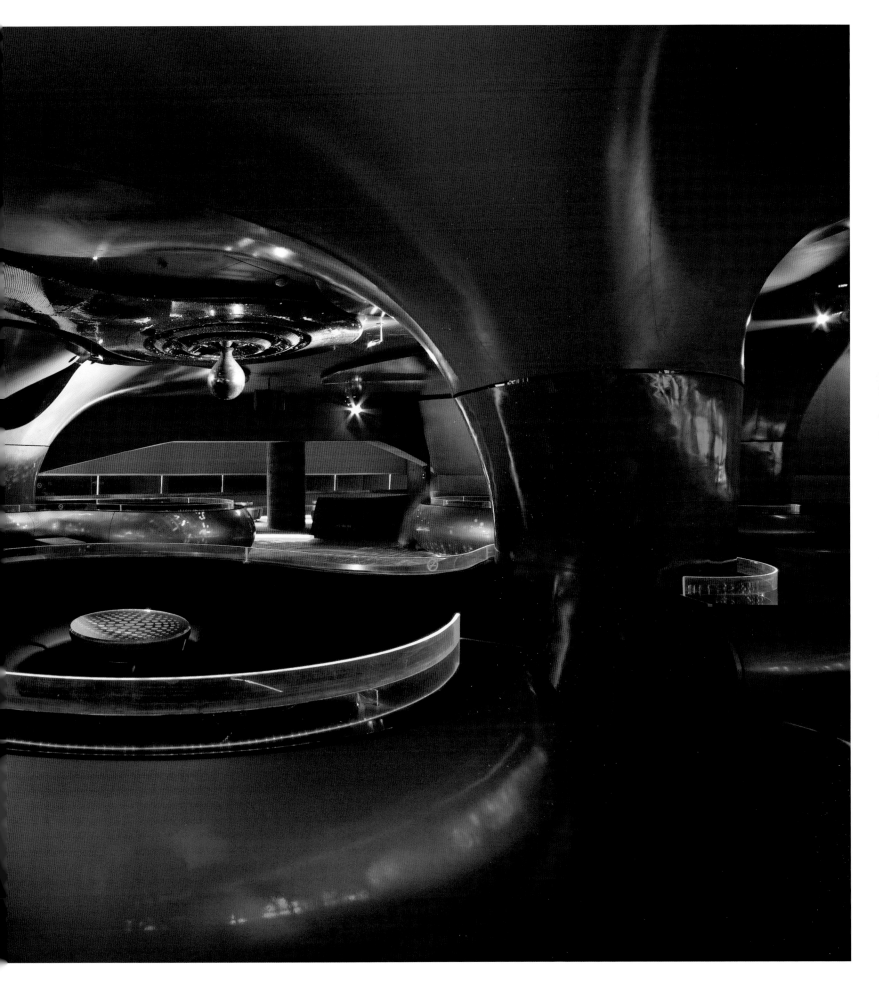

ABOVE
Lines of blue light create rhythm and outline the curved corridor. Amber coloured light from the VIP seating area contrasts with the blue light reflecting off the exposed concrete

LEFT
The design of the seating pods is inspired by the shape of the human ear. A total of five layers of concealed lighting reveal their organic lines

BELOW
The raised DJ booth (first pod from the left) overlooks the entire space, and is also the central hub for controlling the entertainment and architectural lighting

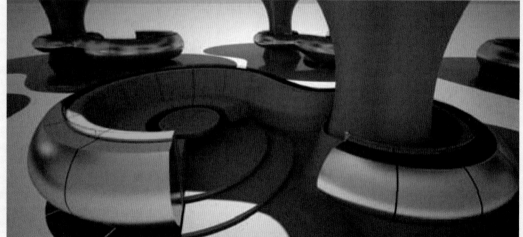

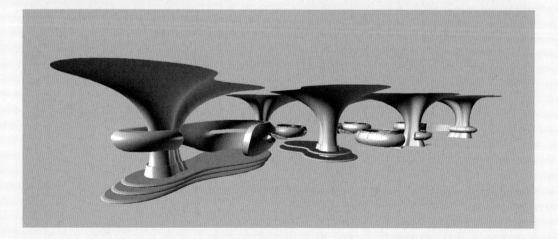

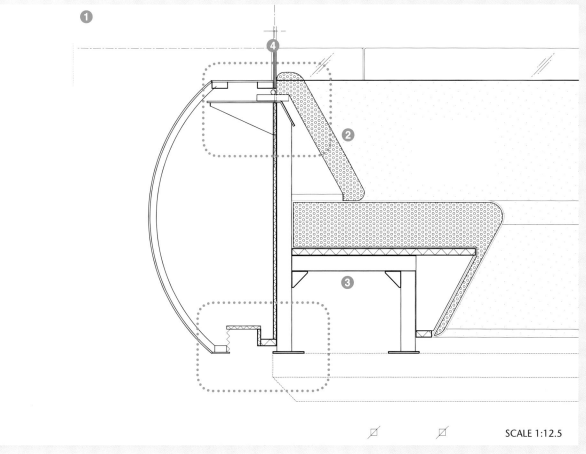

LEFT
Section of seating pod: a steel structure
supports the fibreglass moulding on the
outside and upholstery inside
1 Fibreglass moulding
2 Foam upholstered with fabric
3 Steel structure
4 Clear curved acrylic sheet

SCALE 1:12.5

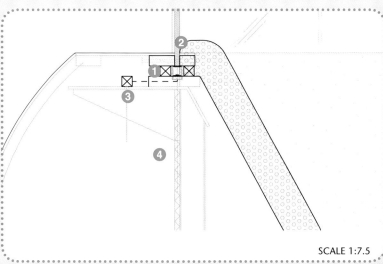

LEFT
Seating pod high-level detail: 10mm (³/₈in)-
thick clear acrylic with frosted edges semi-
recessed at the junction of the upholstery
and fibreglass moulding. Continuous curved-
lensed LEDs illuminate the edge of the acrylic

1 High-output top-emitting blue LEDs
   arranged at the edge of the acrylic to
   create a subtle line of light
2 Curved clear acrylic sheet with
   frosted edges
3 Remote power supplies and DMX
   modules are located on the side of
   the fibreglass moulding and can be
   accessed via a concealed hinge
4 Plywood support

SCALE 1:7.5

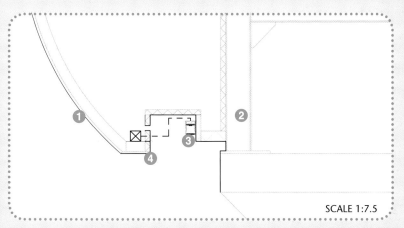

LEFT
Seating pod low-level detail: a recess to
the underside of the fibreglass moulding
conceals a curved-lensed blue LED
striplight to create a floating effect
1 Fibreglass moulding
2 Steel substructure
3 Continuous lensed LED striplight
4 Remote power supplies and DMX
   modules are located behind a concealed
   hinge at the side of the seating

SCALE 1:7.5

LEFT
The corridor from the lift lobby to the main space. Concealed DMX-controlled blue LED striplights, arranged in the joints of the wall and ceiling panels, are programmed to create a breathing or strobe effect. Narrow-beam spots contrast with warm coloured light and create a rhythm of light

BELOW
The 'wall of sound' opposite the lift visualizes the soundwave of the music using LCD screens arranged in the centre. Concealed blue-coloured LED striplights outline the waveform of the front panel

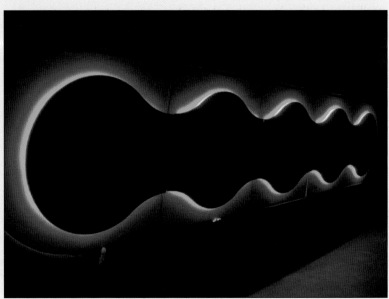

LEFT
Detail section of corridor showing the arrangement of the vertical and horizontal run of blue LEDs

SCALE: 1:33

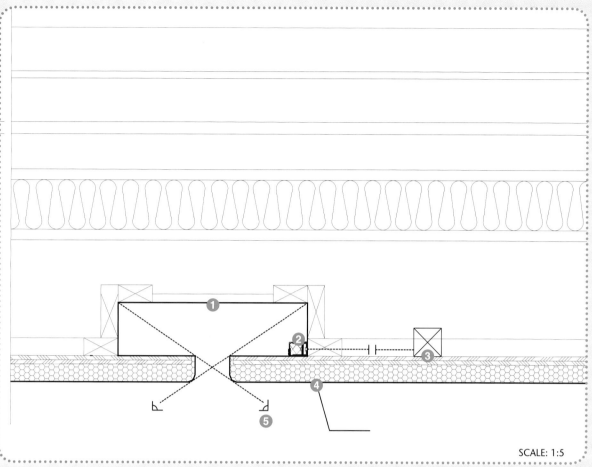

LEFT

Detail section of vertical gap between wall panels

1 Matt light-grey paint finish to the inside

2 DMX-controlled continuous striplight positioned to prevent visibility of the light source

3 Remote power supply and dimmer module located within ceiling void

4 Front fascia of wall panel

5 Line of sight

SCALE: 1:5

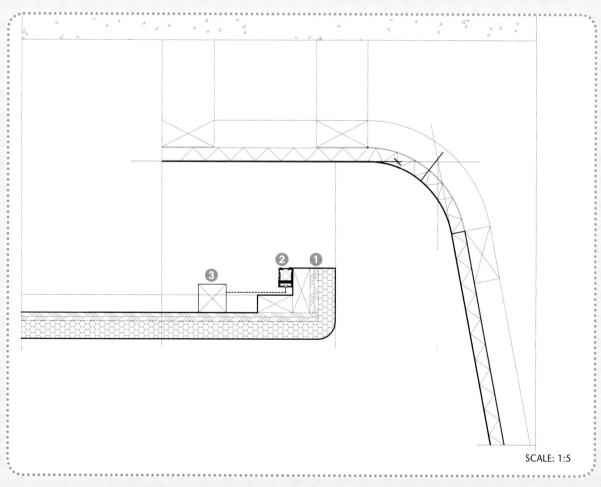

LEFT

Detail section of cove light

1 Upstand to conceal light fixture and control beam spread

2 Continuous blue LED striplight along the edge of the ceiling to reveal the curve of the corridor

3 Remote power supply and dimmer module located within the ceiling cove detail

SCALE: 1:5

RETAIL

ARMANI GINZA TOWER, TOKYO
SPEIRS + MAJOR

Giorgio Armani's flagship store in the Japanese capital not only brings together the group's different brands but also varying types of spaces: the facade, Giorgio Armani (on three floors) and Emporio Armani (sub-ground on two floors) outlets, the first Armani Spa, a restaurant and private bar with roof terrace. While brand differentiation was essential, it was also necessary to create a sense of continuity throughout the building, both from one space to another, and between exterior and interior. This was literally achieved with a light motif.

The gold leaf motif was first developed for the facade in the form of custom LED fittings against a 'bamboo' backcloth. It is translated to a concealed ceiling feature in the Giorgio outlet, to the white light dappling effect of the lift and reiterated in the restaurant, where the golden light of the bamboo leaf is projected with gobo fittings on to the floor and down on to gold tables.

A key use of the concept is in the Giorgio Armani outlet, where it becomes a ceiling light providing the ambient illumination (supplemented by a perimeter light cove and specially designed slot system with CDM-R111 fittings for accenting). Gold-coloured platinum mesh, like floating fabric, is folded inside leaf-shaped apertures – variously 400mm, 570mm and 750mm (15¾in, 22½in and 29½in) long – which conceal overlapping 3000K T5 linear fluorescent lamps, creating a wash of golden light. This effect is echoed by the same gold mesh encapsulated in glass and used as a dividing screen. Lighting control enables a subtle visual trick, dimming and intensifying the tungsten halogen fittings that downlight on to the top edge of the glass so that the mesh becomes more and less solid.

RIGHT

The project's 'light motif' – glimpsed here as the downlight detail in the Giorgio Armani brand outlet – is taken from the facade. 'Bamboo stems' are backlit with 4000K cold cathode and appear to extend up the full height of the building. Interspersed are specially created plastic leaf shapes (750mm x 250mm/ 29½in x 10in), which each have around 150 RGB LED nodes, individually controlled by a video server and media player to produce a twinkling effect

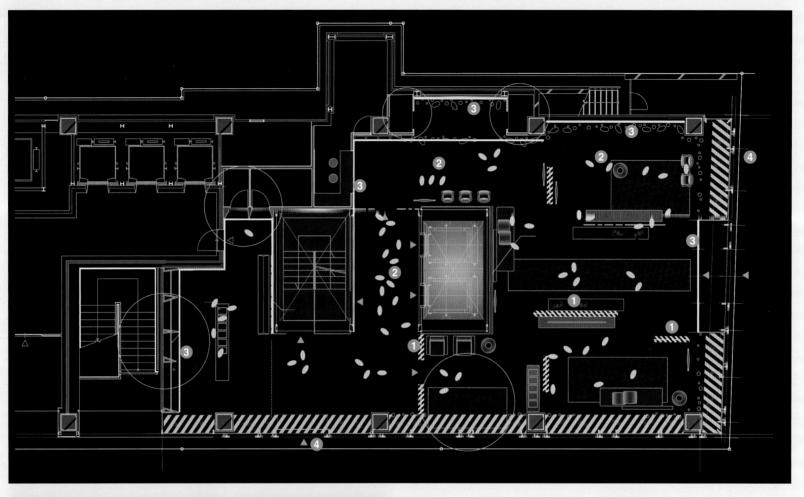

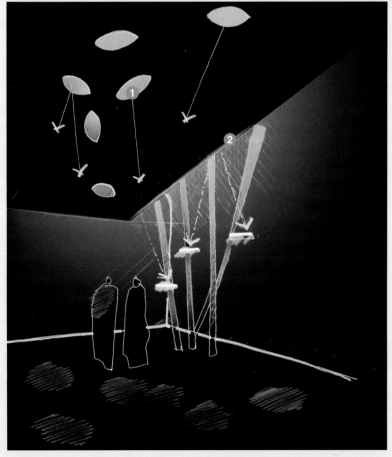

LEFT

Sketch detail of Giorgio Armani outlet

1 Leaf-shaped apertures – 400mm, 570mm and 750mm (15¾in, 22½in and 29½in) long – conceal overlapping 3000K T5 linear fluorescent lamps behind gold-coloured platinum mesh

2 Perimeter cove with concealed tungsten halogen wash lighting to decorative bamboo detail

ABOVE

Plan view of Giorgio Armani outlet

1 Lit glass screen with encapsulated gold mesh

2 Leaf-shaped apertures, backlit with T5 fluorescent lamps

3 Wallwash at cove

4 Oversize slot at bamboo

LEFT AND BELOW LEFT
The gold leaf motif is translated into a variety of lighting techniques throughout the building, including gobo projections on to the floor and tables of the restaurant, and dappled light in the lift

BELOW RIGHT
Plan view of leaf ceiling feature
1 Overlapping 8W 2700K T5 fluorescent lamps
2 50mm (2in) upstand to conceal lamps from view

BOTTOM RIGHT
Section view of leaf ceiling feature
1 Air-conditioning intake
2 Glass fibre-reinforced plastic (GRP)-formed dome mounted above ceiling panel
3 Dome dressed with gold-coloured platinum mesh
4 Leaf-shaped aperture in ceiling
5 T5 lamps mounted out of sight behind 50mm (2in) upstand

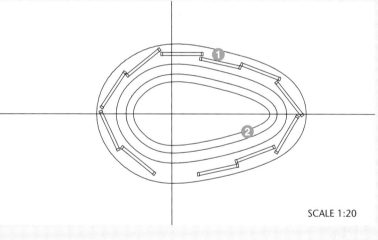

SCALE 1:20

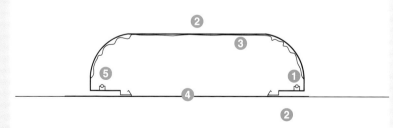

SCALE 1:20

CRYSTALS AT CITYCENTER, LAS VEGAS
FOCUS LIGHTING INC, NY

Located on the famous Las Vegas strip, the Crystals retail centre was designed as a sophisticated urban counterpoint to the surrounding kitsch. The lighting scheme is visually complex, technically advanced, multifaceted and energy efficient (the building has LEED Gold certification and only metal halide, LED and fluorescent sources are used). The two most striking details, which work in conjunction to characterize the central concourse, are the coloured lighting to the ceiling and the dramatic white light slashes on the walls.

In contrast to the typically artificial Las Vegas interior, daylight fills the atrium, which spans 150m (500ft) across and reaches a height of up to 37m (120ft). The angular light slashes that graze across the interior walls not only evoke sunlight passing through skylights, but echo Libeskind's dramatic geometry. The effect is created using 150W theatrical framing metal halide projectors, with precisely adjusted metal shutters, located within specially designed ceiling slots. To reduce ceiling clutter, these same slots also house clamp-mounted fixtures for general area illumination, and metal halide spotlights that highlight various elements of the interior concourse. A scale model and close collaboration with the whole design team allowed the exact location, pitch, length and width of each slot to be calculated and coordinated.

The 15 complex ceiling planes are uplit with coloured light. The concept was to unite the space with subtly shifting tones reminiscent of light reflected off city buildings in an ever-changing rhythm. The varying hues alter the mood of the space and reflect the colour of daylight outside. Creating these effects are around 1,000 colour-changing fixtures housed on the walls and ceiling ledges. The colour washing combines RGB (red, green, blue) fittings and AW (amber and white) fittings focused on the same spot to get precise pastel shades not achievable with RGB fixtures alone. To achieve the extraordinary precision, photometric software, 3D models and full-scale mock-ups were all used to verify throw distances, beam spreads and aiming angles prior to construction. Once installed, each fixture was precisely aimed and accessorized with diffusion films to ensure an even blend across the compound curves of the multiple ceiling planes.

RIGHT
In a visually complex and highly precise scheme, slashes of light from slot-mounted metal halide projectors combine with colour washes from LEDs. This is a view up towards the complex ceiling planes that are highlighted with contrasting colours.

RIGHT
Reflected ceiling plan showing enlarged
detail of ceiling slot
1 Wall slashes
2 General area lighting
3 Feature lighting, grand stair floor pattern
and colour

OPPOSITE
Reflected ceiling plan showing positions
of slots providing white light wall slashes,
plus general and feature lighting
1 Position of section detail shown on
this page
2 Position of section detail shown on
page 158

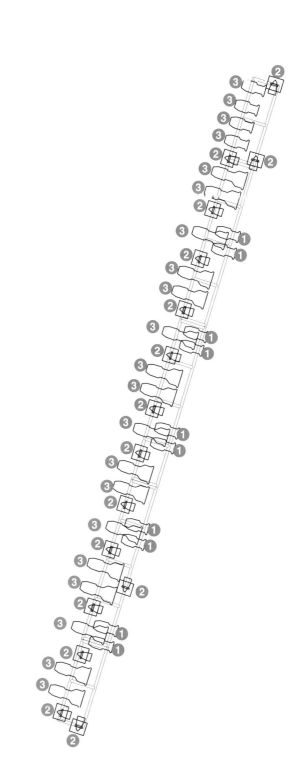

SCALE 1:50

SCALE 1:150

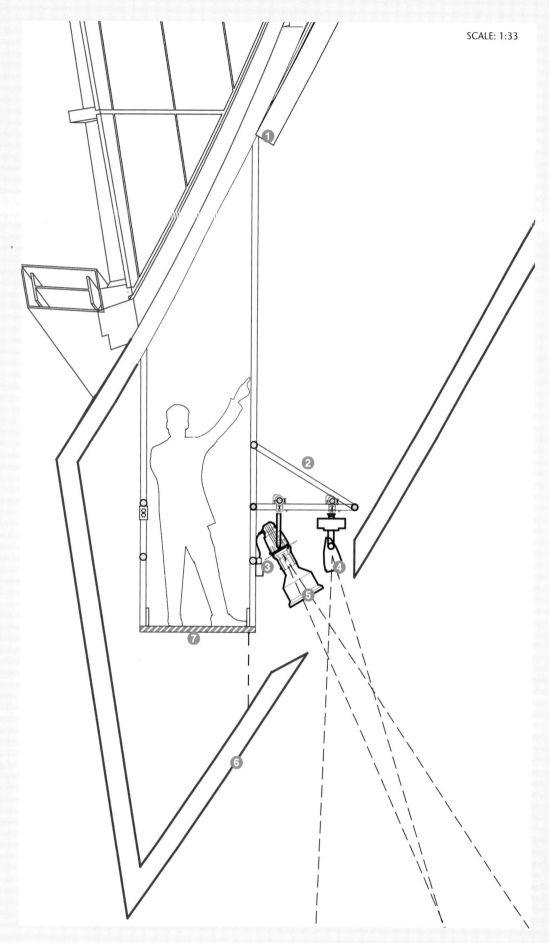

LEFT

1 Roof structure

2 Continuous steel pipe structure cantilevered off catwalk to support clamp-mounted light fixtures

3 Custom-made plugging strip raceway with twist-lock receptacles for power to light fixtures

4 Clamp-mounted 150W metal halide spotlight with very narrow optical reflector to provide general area lighting to concourse 30m (98ft) below

5 Clamp-mounted 150W metal halide theatrical framing projector for accent lighting on special features within concourse (wide range of accessories used to control beam width and colour for different applications)

6 Ceiling plane

7 Catwalk, hung from roof trussing, for maintenance access

LEFT

Section view of RGB (red, green, blue) and WWA (white, white, amber) LED fixtures paired on ceiling ledges and walls to create exact pastel colours on the ceiling. Glare-shielded accessories and louvres minimize direct view of LEDs while optical spread lenses vary beam spread from 10 to 60 degrees

1 Skylight
2 Surface-mounted warm white floodlight uplighting ceiling
3 Recessed pocket with ventilated access panel to house remote data enablers
4 Surface-mounted RGB colour-change LED floodlight uplighting ceiling
5 Power and data wires
6 Sides open to plenum for ventilation
7 Recessed junction box

BELOW

The complex geometry of the 37m (120ft) high space is accentuated using colour on the compound curve ceiling planes and patterns of light on the angled wall. Photometric software, 3D models and full-scale mock-ups were needed to achieve precise throw distances, beam spreads and aiming angles

SCALE 1:25

ION ORCHARD, SINGAPORE
LIGHTING PLANNERS ASSOCIATES & PARSONS BRINCKERHOFF

ION Orchard is a landmark retail development and gateway to one of Singapore's most sophisticated shopping areas at the intersection of Orchard and Scotts Road. With 60,000sq m (645,000sq ft) across eight floors and 335 shops, the mall was also envisaged as a social hub, and artistic activities are a large part of its agenda.

Signalling both its artistic ambition and epitomizing the vibrancy of this retail and entertainment hub, an RGB colour-changing LED media facade wraps around the powerful curved form of the 117m (384ft) glass frontage. This showcases the mall's retail brands, as well as serving as a fluid canvas for multimedia art and live telecasts of events held within the complex. It can also screen live global events. While most media walls are only concerned with their external face, the aim here was to use a system that would not interrupt the view through the glass. At night the view from the inside is designed to be as impressive as the media art reflected across the exterior facade.

A further aim was to create vibrancy without vulgarity. This was achieved less from the technology than the content, which is designed to be meaningful to local people and also involve local artists who are regularly invited to recreate it. The massive media wall is divided into three different types, each fulfilling a different function. One section, facing the event plaza at the main entrance, is used as a TV screen. The second section is used as an artistic canvas and features lower LED resolution, enough for the creation of abstract images. The third application of the LEDs is to mark the structural joints and express the organic form of the podium building.

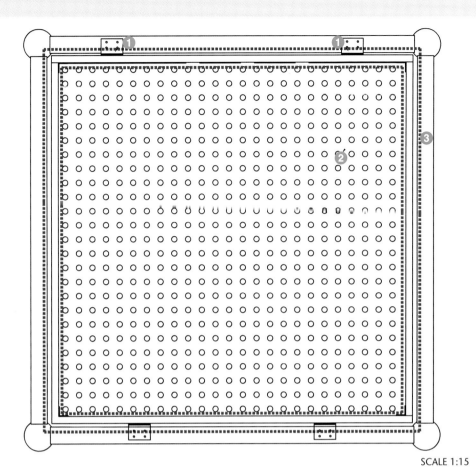

LEFT
Detail of the TV screen element of the
LED facade (back view)
1 Panel bracket
2 Perforated aluminium back cover
3 RHS/SHS space frame

BELOW
Elevation detail of TV screen element
1 Self-tapping screw
2 SHS
3 Cap screw for aluminium bracket
4 Aluminium bracket for mounting panels
5 LED strip mounted to frame
6 Glass
7 LED strip
8 Aluminium LED frame

SCALE 1:15

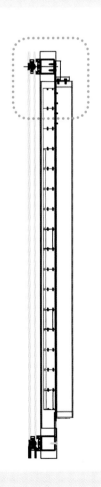

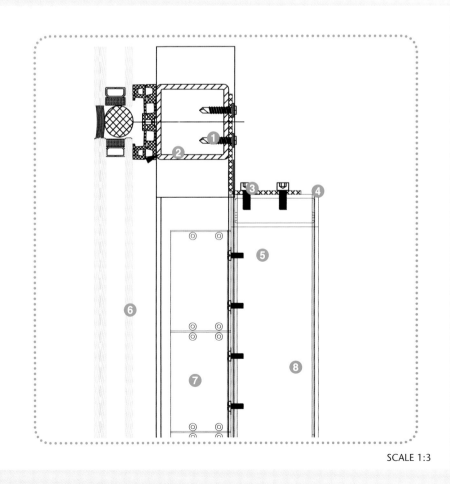

SCALE 1:3

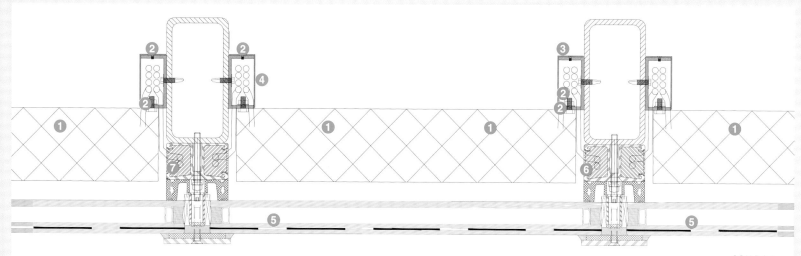

SCALE 1:3

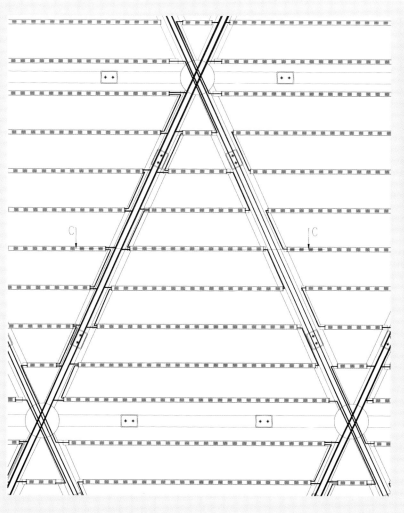

TOP
Section detail of artistic canvas element
of LED facade where resolution is just
sufficient for abstract images
1 LED fitting
2 Mounting screws
3 Aluminium mounting frame
4 Aluminium cover plate
5 Glass
6 Conduit for data cable
7 Conduit for power cable

ABOVE
Unusually for a media facade, the effects
are visible from the interior

LEFT
Detail of artistic canvas element of
LED facade

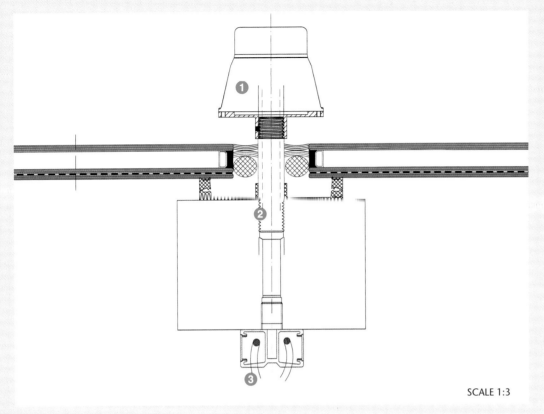

LEFT
Section view of LED fitting marking
structural joints on double-glazed section
1 RGB LED spotlight
2 MS galvanized threaded sleeve
3 Cable trunking

BELOW
Front view of LED spotlight at
structural joint
1 Steel node
2 Structural steel, rectangular
  hollow section
3 RGB LED spotlight

SCALE 1:3

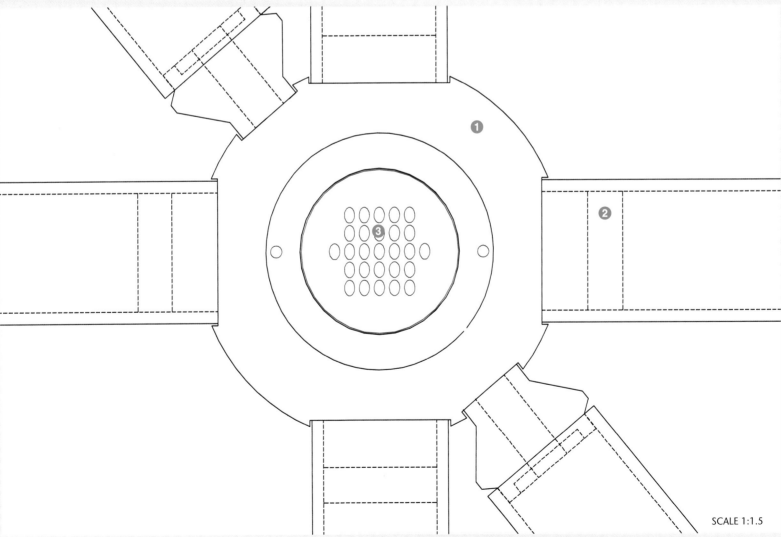

SCALE 1:1.5

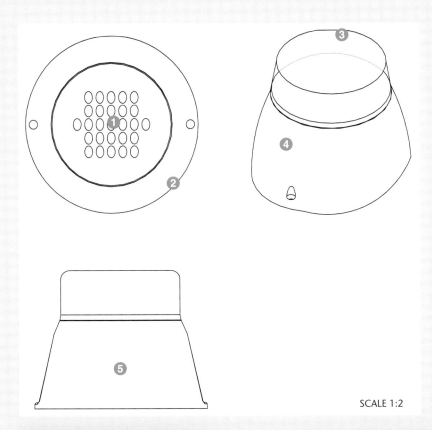

LEFT
Top, isometric and side views of
LED spotlight
1 RGB LEDs (4, 9, 12 per pixel)
2 Diameter 100mm (4in)
3 UV-stabilized polycarbonate diffuser
4 Powder-coated cast aluminium
5 Height 70mm (2¾in)

BELOW
The third application of LEDs on the
facade is to mark the points of structural
joints and express the organic form of
the podium building

SCALE 1:2

ITSU SUSHI, TERMINAL 5, HEATHROW AIRPORT, LONDON
CINIMOD STUDIO

Butterfly in Flight is the culmination of a series of artworks commissioned by Julian Metcalfe, founder of UK food chain Pret a Manger, and Itsu sushi restaurants and takeaways. A snaking three-dimensional sculpture based on the Itsu logo, it has 45 wing pairs that change dynamically in shape and angle to convey the stages of a butterfly's flight. The wings are mounted on a three dimensionally curved polished aluminium spine structure that arches and bends through space, reaching heights of between 3m and 5m (10ft and 16ft).

Advanced parametric techniques helped capture key moments in the ephemeral motion of a butterfly, with each CNC-cut component following the form of a wing – ranging from 75cm to 200cm (29½in to 78¾in) – as it twists and unfurls during flight. The material is a BAA-approved sheet polycarbonate (the acrylic-based Prismex that had been used on an earlier version of the artwork wasn't allowed because of fire safety concerns in the airside location).

Elegant curved grooves, created with bespoke parametric software, are custom-etched to the front face of each wing to achieve a smooth lighting effect. The CNC-cut depth of each groove varies across the panel, getting deeper towards the centres in order to capture maximum light. White LEDs, rebated in a 4mm ($^1/_6$ in)-deep channel CNC-cut into the 6mm (¼in)-thick polycarbonate, run the full perimeter of each wing. The density is 120 LEDs per metre (20W), with 240 LEDs used on the larger wing pairs. A combination of light transmission and the reflection caused by dichroic film on the back face of each wing creates a subtle kaleidoscopic colour shift that alters with the viewer's position. A custom lighting control system was also designed to animate the artwork. This includes gentle ripples of light movements, accentuated by larger and more noticeable 'butterfly flutters'.

RIGHT
Embedded with white LEDs, the three-dimensional sculpture captures key moments in a butterfly's flight

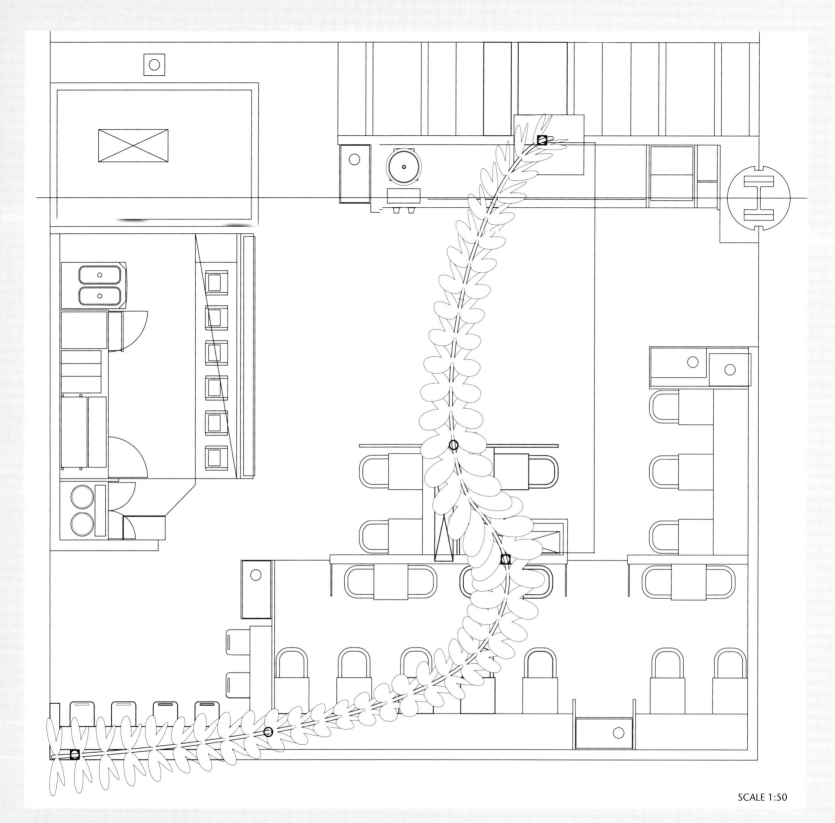

SCALE 1:50

ABOVE
Plan view of sculpture, which arches
and bends through the space, reaching
heights of between 3m and 5m (10ft
and 16ft)

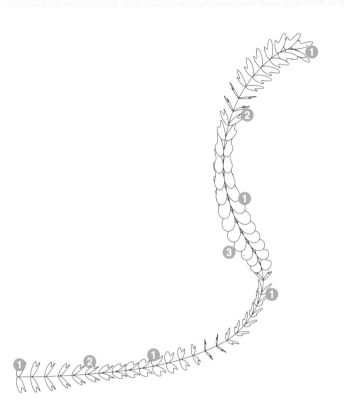

SCALE 1:100

ABOVE
Overall wing layout
1 Structural fixing points
2 Highest points 5m (16ft)
3 Lowest points 3m (10ft)

ABOVE
Light transmission combined with the reflection caused by dichroic film on the back face of each wing creates a kaleidoscopic colour shift that alters with the viewer's position

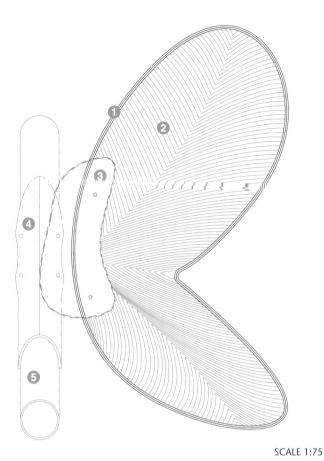

SCALE 1:75

LEFT
Interface of wing and bracket
1 Inset LED groove
2 Polycarbonate wing with
groove pattern
3 Wing clamp
4 Wing bracket
5 Supporting polished aluminium
tubular structure

BELOW
Curved grooves, created with bespoke
parametric software, are custom-etched
to the front face of each wing to achieve
a smooth lighting effect. The CNC cut
depth of each groove varies across the
panel, getting deeper towards the centres
to capture maximum light

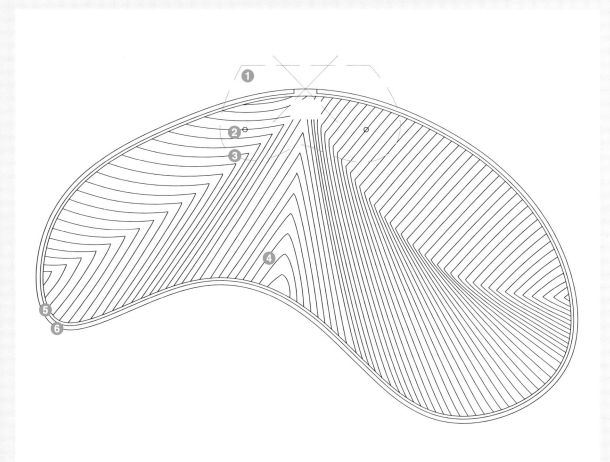

LEFT
Typical wing detail
1 Bracket tolerance region
2 Bracket bolt hole 5mm ($^1/_5$in) diameter
3 Bracket
4 Groove pattern depth 1–2mm
($^1/_{25}$–$^1/_{12}$in)
5 Wing LED groove 4mm ($^1/_6$in),
depth 4.5mm ($^1/_6$in)
6 Wing lip 6mm (¼in)

BELOW
Each CNC-cut component follows the
form of a wing, ranging from 75cm
to 200cm (29½in to 78¾in)

SCALE 1:4

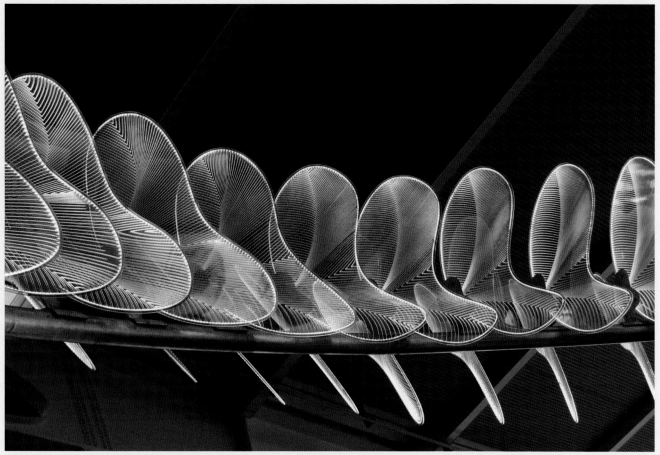

JOYERÍA D JEWELLERY OUTLET PAMPLONA
ALS LIGHTING

An antidote to the cluttered traditional jeweller, Joyería D has a stark, geometric interior designed to play with light and shadow, providing a theatrical setting for the jewellery. Deep, narrow and just 30sq m (323sq ft), the shop concept recalls a coffer. The interior comprises two sections: the top is dark, matt, light and soft, while the bottom – the floor, half-height wall behind the counter and display box doors are made of large smelted-aluminium slabs – is at once silvery, heavy and rigid.

While halogen, notable for its warmth, sparkle and crispness, is usually associated with jewellery outlets, all the sources are cool white and low energy. LEDs are used for accenting the jewellery items while linear fluorescent draws a line of light where planes meet. The shop floor and counter are lit by narrow-beam metal halide spots surface-mounted within the ceiling ribs. Barn doors allow precise light control. High-output linear fluorescent fixtures at the base of the counter create a floating effect.

The semi-recessed display boxes behind the counter are hidden behind doors. The box interiors are lit from within using an L-shaped LED profile. High-output linear fluorescent luminaires hidden behind the curtain-like dark wall light their exterior. On the facing wall, jewellery exhibited in the display boxes is illuminated by compact fluorescent lamps (CFLs) which also highlight the base of the walls.

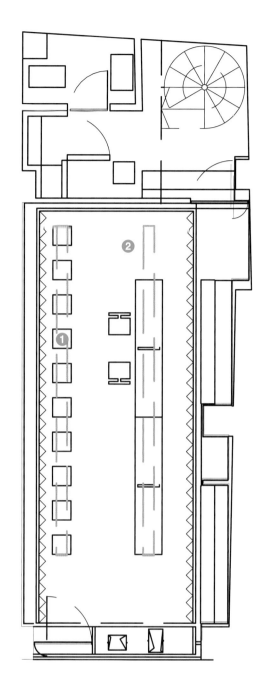

SCALE 1:75

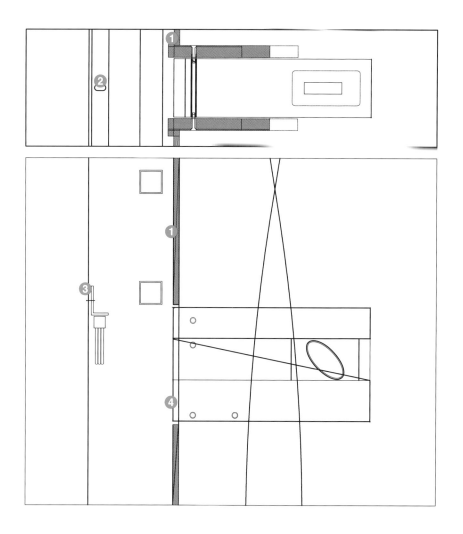

SCALE 1:5

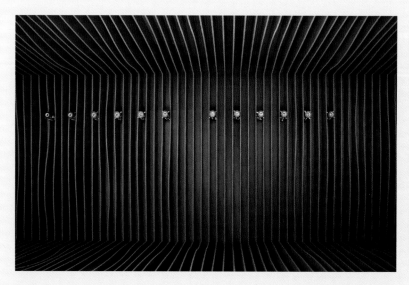

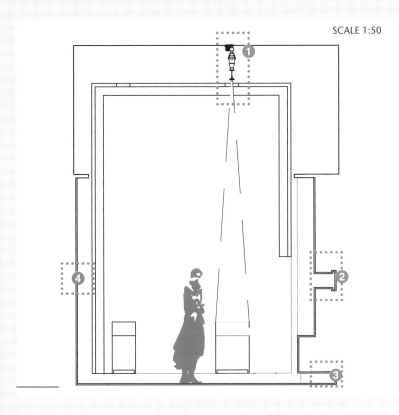

SCALE 1:50

LEFT
Section showing position of various
light sources
1 Track-mounted metal halide spots
2 Semi-recessed display boxes backlit
with LEDs
3 High-output fluorescent
4 Methacrylate display box backlit
with CFL

BELOW LEFT
Detail 1
Track-mounted, narrow-beam metal
halide spots provide tightly controlled
light to the counter surface

BELOW CENTRE
Detail 2
Semi-recessed display boxes backlit with
customized L-profile LED fixture

BELOW RIGHT TOP
Detail 3
High-output fluorescent illuminates the
exterior of the semi-recessed display
boxes and creates a floating effect for
the counter

BELOW RIGHT BOTTOM
Detail 4
A compact fluorescent lamp backlights
the methacrylate display box and also
illuminates the foot of the wall

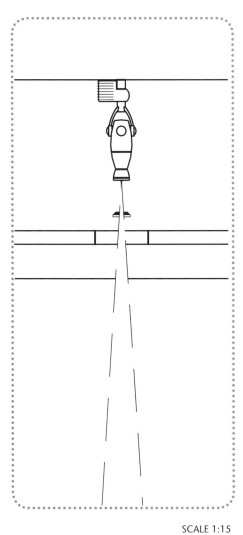

SCALE 1:15

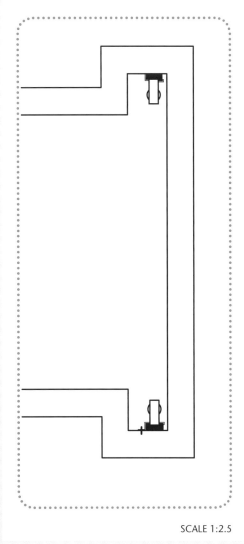

SCALE 1:2.5

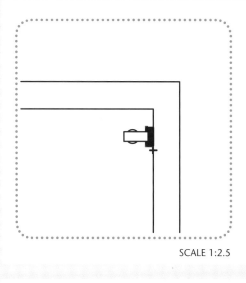

SCALE 1:2.5

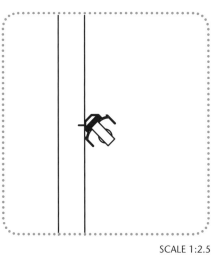

SCALE 1:2.5

MIZU HAIRDRESSING SALON, BOSTON
PARSONS BRINCKERHOFF

The Mizu Salon is part of Boston's six-star Mandarin Oriental Hotel complex. The interior comprises a series of vaults in two directions. The resulting forms partly screen the clients from pedestrian mall traffic while attracting potential customers with fleeting views of styling activity and the unusual interior. Detailed computer modelling helped the designers and owners visualize and adjust the balance of ambient, accent and task lighting. Illuminance is highest at the styling stations and gradually diminishes towards the washing sinks and corridor, where the tasks are less exacting.

The primary aim was to create an environment that was calm and uplifting, and which literally put clients in a flattering light. The scheme uses strategic reflective lighting and lightboxes, and relies on the complete integration of light and architecture for its impact. The simple vaulted cutting/styling room is animated by rhythmic cuts in the gypsum soffit, with light emanating from openings where the shapes intersect and part. Cool colour temperatures (fluorescent) are used to create a sense of calm and cleanliness, countered by warm, gold colours (tungsten halogen) for relaxation and comfort.

In this main styling space, the openings in the gypsum shapes hold acrylic diffusing material behind which linear fluorescent lighting, CRI 80-plus, emphasizes the continuous smooth white surfaces of the vaults and floor while softly lighting clients' faces and hair. Behind the mirrors compact fluorescent strips fit in the narrow space between the acrylic sheet and the wall. The mirror in the centre appears to float on the diffuser, with the practical effect of providing even, flattering illumination to the client's face, with no shadowing.

Low-voltage recessed adjustable spots – with low-brightness, flangeless trims around 6cm (2½in) in diameter – are discreetly positioned at the apex of the sweeping forms. These accent hair for cutting and styling without creating glare. The components of the scheme can be switched separately to adapt to different conditions and the occasional event.

RIGHT
Using strategic reflective lighting and lightboxes, the scheme relies on the complete integration of light and architecture for its impact

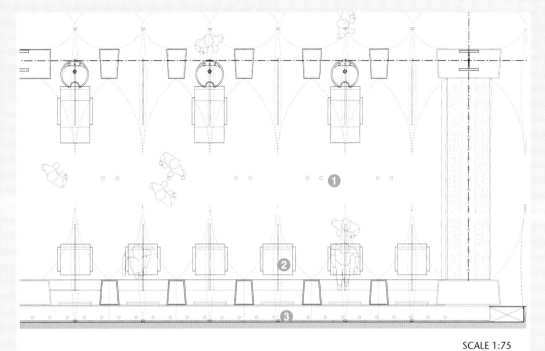

LEFT
Plan view showing fittings in styling area
(and in corridor behind)
1 LV adjustable accent fitting
2 T8 strip fluorescent at oculus
3 Lightbox with CFL backlighting mirror

BELOW
In the cutting/styling area, diffused
fluorescent provides a flattering, even
light to the face, while ceiling-recessed
LV tungsten halogen fittings provide
task lighting

SCALE 1:75

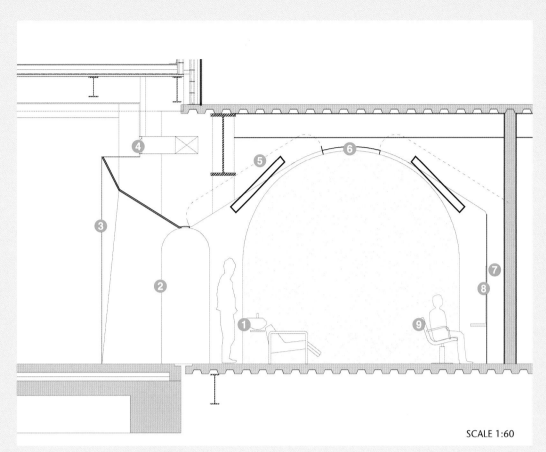

LEFT
Section of washing/cutting area
1 Washbasin
2 Corridor
3 Glazing
4 Diffuser
5 T8 fluorescent behind acrylic diffuser
6 LV adjustable accent fitting
7 Lightbox with CFL backlighting mirror
8 Mirror
9 Cutting station

SCALE 1:60

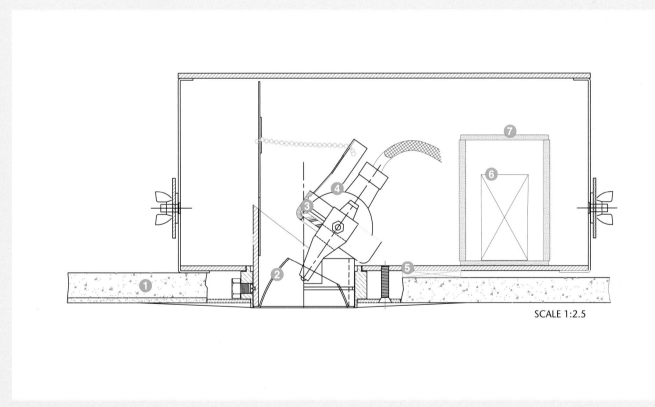

SCALE 1:2.5

ABOVE
Section detail of LV recessed adjustable
accent fitting
1 Gypsum board
2 Clear anodized-finish aluminium cone
3 Solite lens
4 12V MR16 lamp (max 65W)
5 Spacer
6 Transformer
7 Wiring chamber

MURALE BEAUTY RETAIL OUTLET, MONTREAL
BURDIFILEK

Murale in Montreal is one of a recently launched chain of prestige beauty shops which combine luxury cosmetic, fragrance and skin care collections with a pharmacy and personalized beauty services. The 750sq m (8,000sq ft) shop interior is designed to set a benchmark for this new 'cosmeceutical' retail concept in the Canadian market. Lighting was an important component of the white, sculptural space, which aspires to a gallery atmosphere, avoiding conventions such as aisles to encourage a sense of discovery.

Two specific lighting details help define the space and also act as focal points to draw the customer through. Clear Starfire glass LED-lit 'fins' define the dermatology area and act as a focal point in the rear of the shop. Measuring 350cm (138in) high, the 2cm (¾in)-thick, wave-shaped glass fins, 30 in all, are positioned 100mm (4in) apart to form a curved boundary. These are accented with a warm white (3000K) LED strip installed in a metal chanel at the rear of each fin. The glass is sandblasted both in front of the LEDs, to soften the pinpoint effect of the individual diodes, and at the outer edge to produce a more diffused effect as light is transmitted edge-on through the glass.

The 19m (62ft)-long back wall is defined by a kinetic light installation: a backlit LED 'waterfall'. Warm white (3400K) LED strips were installed at various intervals in a vertical 'barcode' pattern at a 2.5cm (1in) distance behind sandblasted Lucite acrylic panels. Constructed in 150cm (59in) segments, the plywood vertical behind the acrylic panels has slots for the LEDs, which are also visible in between display shelves mounted on the bottom half. Where possible the LEDs were positioned on the butt seams of the acrylic panels to create a smoother, more uniform effect across the wall. Each strip is individually programmed to run a continuous pattern, creating the effect of raindrops or water trickling down a windowpane.

RIGHT
Two lighting details – LED-lit glass fins and a kinetic LED lighting effect on the back wall – both define the space and draw customers through

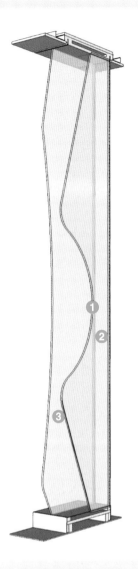

PERSPECTIVE

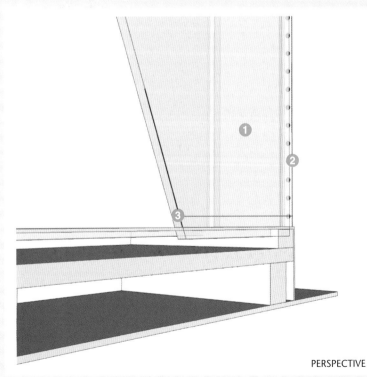

PERSPECTIVE

LEFT
Detail of glass fin
1 2cm (¾in)-thick Starfire glass fin
2 Warm white LED strip in metal channel
3 Sandblasted edge

BELOW LEFT
Detail of glass fin at base
1 2cm (¾in)-thick Starfire glass fin
2 Warm white LED strip in metal channel
3 Sandblasted edge

BELOW
The glass fins are sandblasted in front of
the LEDs to soften their pinpoint effect,
and also at the outer edge, resulting in a
more diffused effect as light is transmitted
edge-on through the glass

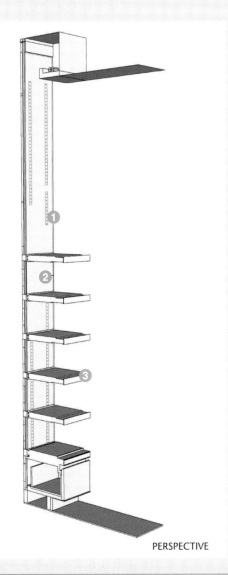

PERSPECTIVE

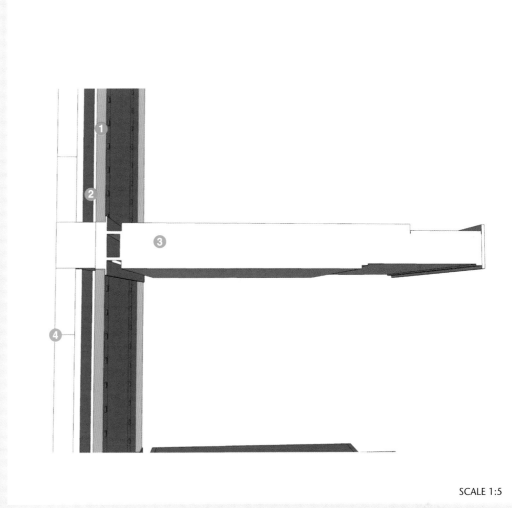

SCALE 1:5

ABOVE LEFT
Detail of 150cm (59in) back wall section
1 Warm white LED strip on programmed
loop behind acrylic panel
2 1.25cm (½in) sandblasted Lucite
acrylic panel
3 Display shelf on lower half of wall

TOP RIGHT
Detail of 150cm (59in) back wall section
1 1.25cm (½in) sandblasted Lucite
acrylic panel
2 Warm white LED strip on programmed
loop behind acrylic panel
3 Display shelf
4 Plywood panel

LEFT
Each LED strip is individually
programmed, creating the effect of
raindrops down a windowpane

SNOG FROZEN YOGURT, LONDON/INTERNATIONAL
CINIMOD STUDIO

Starting as a small outlet in London, the Snog frozen yogurt chain is now spreading out across South America, Europe and the Middle East. Essential to its brand identity are its dynamic lit ceilings, which rely on cutting edge technology and which have evolved from an animated sky effect to the latest incarnation, an undulating, rainbow-coloured LED canopy.

Formed using parametric software, the ceiling is made from CNC-cut mirrored panels with a stretch diffuser across the bottom, and varies in depth and pitch. Specially designed and fabricated RGBW LED battens form a 'ladder' grid within each of the ribbons. There are 400 strips, all individually controlled, spaced at 13cm (5in) centres. RGBW LEDs were used as the additional white light provides a higher colour control and rendering. This allows for more natural colours, including sky blues that are not as saturated as they would be with RGB LEDs alone.

The intricate, dynamic lighting effects are achieved with a new lighting control system, a customized version of amBX's amBIENT XC DMX controller, that approaches complex lighting sequences in a completely different way. RGB LEDs usually need extensive programming. Using this embedded technology, the amBX controller takes real-time audio and video feeds and uses the content to control them, allowing instant and constantly changing lighting effects to be created in real time without lengthy programming. In this case it responds to a music soundtrack. The effects are never repeated as the system evolves and builds on itself.

RIGHT
The intricate coloured lighting effects of the undulating ceiling are achieved with a new approach to lighting control

LEFT
The first version of the ceiling was developed for the King's Road, London, outlet

BELOW
Section view

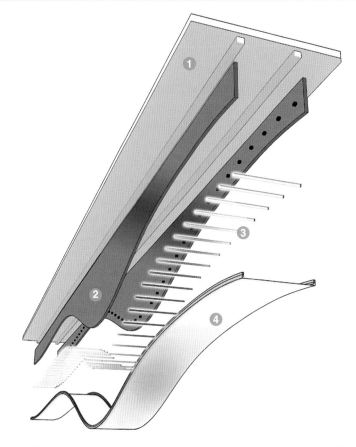

ABOVE
RGBW LED battens, specially designed and made, form a 'ladder' grid within each of the ribbons. There are 400 strips, all individually controlled, spaced at 13cm (5in) centres

LEFT
Ceiling detail
1 Ceiling structure
2 CNC-cut MDF profiles with laminated mirror finish
3 Individually controllable RGBW LED battens
4 Stretch translucent ceiling

RESOURCES

DIRECTORY OF ARCHITECTS

AUSTRIA

Bartenbach LichtLabor GmbH
Rinner Strasse 14
6071 Aldrans/Tyrol
T +43 512 3338-0
F +43 512 3338-88
info@bartenbach.com
www.bartenbach.com
Bridge Pavilion, Zaragoza

Zumtobel Lighting GmbH
Head Office
Schweizer Strasse 30
A-6851 Dornbirn
T +43 5572 390-0
F +43 5572 22826
info@zumtobel.info
www.zumtobel.com
Ropemaker Place

DENMARK

Studio Steven Scott
Frydenlundsvej 55
2950 Vedbæk
T +45 27112358
sss@stevenscott.dk
www.studiostevenscott.com
Deloitte HQ

FRANCE

Light Cibles
16 Passage Charles Dallery
75011 Paris
T +33 (0)1 53 27 60 34
F +33 (0)1 53 27 60 27
www.light-cibles.com
**Satellite 4, Charles De Gaulle
Airport; CNIT**

GERMANY

Licht Kunst Licht AG
D-53115 Bonn
Jagdweg 16
T +49 (0) 228 914 220
F +49 (0) 228 911 244
bonn@lichtkunstlicht.com
www.lichtkunstlicht.de
**ENBW City; Assembly Hall
Liechtenstein Parliament**

Pfarré Lighting Design
Sonnentaustrasse 12
80995 München
T +49 (0) 89 540 41 43-0
F +49 (0) 89 540 41 43-43
info@lichtplanung.com
www.lichtplanung.com
Palace of International Forums

GREECE

L+DG
Thomas Gravanis Lighting
Architects
23-25 Kleomenous Street
Athens 10676
T +30 210 7254896
F +30 210 7234408
info@lightingdg.com
www.lightingdg.com
Chan Restaurant; The Met Hotel

JAPAN

LightDesign Inc.
2-11-18-4F Ginza, Chuo-ku
Tokyo, Japan 104-0061
T +81 3 3545 6339
F +81 3 3545 6329
lightdesign@lightdesign.jp
www.lightdesign.jp
Za-Koenji Public Theatre

Lighting Planners Associates
5-28-10, Jingumae, Shibuya-ku
Tokyo, Japan 150-0001
T +81 3 5469 1022
F +81 3 5469 1023
lpa@lighting.co.jp
www.lighting.co.jp
Ion Orchard

SPAIN

ALS Lighting
C/ San Mateo, 12 10 Centro
CP 28004 Madrid
F +34 944 104 751
T +34 696 914 935
info@alslighting.com
www.alslighting.com
Joyería D Jewellery Outlet

TAIWAN

CMA Lighting Design Inc.
7F, No. 55, Lane 100, Tun-Hwa
South Road #1, Taipe
T +886-2-27417271
F +886-2-27785256
cmalighting@seed.net.tw
www.cmalighting.com.tw
**Ruentex Tunhua-Renai
Condominium**

UK

Arup
8 Fitzroy Street
London W1T 4BJ
T +44 (0) 20 7755 5802/4
F +44 (0) 20 7755 2561
info@arupassociates.com
www.arupassociates.com
**Ropemaker Place; The Modern
Wing, Art Institute of Chicago;
Parthenon Gallery, Acropolis
Museum**

Cinimod Studio Ltd
Unit 304, Westbourne Studios
242 Acklam Road
London W10 5JJ
T +44 (0) 20 8969 3960
enquiries@cinimodstudio.com
www.cinimodstudio.com
**Itsu Sushi, Heathrow Airport;
Snog Frozen Yogurt**

dpa lighting design
Unit 228, 30 Great Guildford Street
London, SE1 0HS
T +44 (0) 20 3142 6300
F +44 (0) 20 3002 2704
london@dpalighting.com
www.dpalighting.com
Espa at the Europe Hotel

Elektra Lighting
3rd Floor, 6 Dyers Buildings
Holborn, London EC1N 2JT
T +44 (0) 20 7288 0155
F +44 (0) 20 7359 8788
info@elektralighting.co.uk
www.elektralighting.co.uk
The Studio, Andaz Hotel

Inverse Lighting Design
1A Peacock Yard
Iliffe Street, London SE17 3LH
T +44 (0)20 7708 2749
ldn@inverselighting.co.uk
www.inverselighting.co.uk
Sound Nightclub

Isometrix Lighting + Design
8 Glasshouse Yard
London EC1A 4JNT
T +44 (0) 20 7253 2888
F +44 (0) 20 7253 2899
ltg@isometrix.co.uk
www.isometrix.co.uk
Opposite House Hotel

Jason Bruges Studio
Green Mews
Bevenden Street
London N1 6AS
T +44 20 7490 4590
F +44 20 7490 0555
info@jasonbruges.com
www.jasonbruges.com
Platform 5 Sunderland Station

Light Bureau Limited
7F Hewlett House
Havelock Terrace
London SW8 4AS
T +44 (0)20 7498 6111
F +44 (0)20 7498 6408
mail@lightbureau.com
www.lightbureau.com
KPMG HQ

Light + Design Associates
Studio G7, Lafone House
The Leather Market
Weston Street
London SE1 3ER
T +44 (0) 20 7403 4700
design@lightanddesign.co.uk
www.lightanddesign.co.uk
**Convention/Banqueting Facility,
Qatar National Convention
Centre**

Lighting Design International Ltd
3 Hammersmith Studios
55a Yeldham Road, London W6 8JF
T +44 (0) 20 8600 5777
F +44 (0) 20 8600 5778
design@ldi-uk.com
www.lightingdesigninternational.com
Private Residential Spa

Maurice Brill Lighting Design Ltd.
82 Rivington Street
London EC2A 3AZ
T +44 (0)20 7729 5633
F +44 (0)20 7729 5644
mail@mbld.co.uk
www.mbld.co.uk
133 Houndsditch

MindsEye
Unit 19 Hiltongrove
14 Southgate Road
London N1 3LY
T +44 (0)20 7923 0508
F +44 (0)20 7923 0509
mail@mindseye3d.com
www.mindseye3d.com
The Rotunda

SAS International
T +44 (0) 118 929 0900
enquiries@sasint.co.uk
www.sasint.co.uk
Ropemaker Place

Speirs + Major
11-15 Emerald Street
London WC1N 3QL
T +44 (0) 20 7067 4700
F +44 (0) 20 7067 4701
info@speirsandmajor.com
www.speirsandmajor.com
**Sheikh Zayed Bin Sultan Al
Nahyan Mosque; Armani
Ginza Tower**

Stortford Interiors (UK) Limited
Unit 1, Twyford Business Centre
London Road, Herts. CM23 3YT
Bishop's Stortford
T +44 (0)1279 714600
F +44 (0)1279 714699
victoria@stortford-interiors.com
www.stortford-interiors.com
Ropemaker Place

NORTH AMERICA

BURDIFILEK
183 Bathurst Street
Suite 300
Toronto, ON M5T 2R7
Canada
T +1 416 703 4334
info@burdifilek.com
www.burdifilek.co
Murale Beauty Retail Outlet

CANDELA
720 Olive Way, Suite 1400
Seattle, Washington 98101
T +1 206 667 0511
F +1 206 667 0512
connect@candela.com
www.candela.com
**The Lightcatcher, Whatcom
Museum**

**Cline Bettridge Bernstein
Lighting Design Inc.**
30 West 22nd Street, 4th Floor
New York, NY 10010
T +1 212 741 3280
F +1 212 741 3112
sbernstein@cbbld.com
www.cbbld.com
**GSC Group Offices; Renée and
Henry Segerstrom Concert Hall**

Derek Porter Studio
1907 Wyandotte Trafficway
Kansas City, Missouri 64108
T +1 816 842 9060
F +1 816 842 9061
anne@derekporterstudio.com
www.derekporterstudio.com
Private Residence, Missouri

Elliott + Associates Architects
35 Harrison Avenue
Oklahoma City
Oklahoma 73104
T +1 405 232 9554
F +1 405 232 9997
design@e-a-a.com
www.e-a-a.com
Car Park One, Chesapeake Energy

Focus Lighting, Inc.
221 West 116th Street
New York, NY 10026
T +1 212 865 1565
F +1 212 865 4217
info@focuslighting.com
www.focuslighting.com
Crystals at CityCenter Las Vegas

**Horton Lees Brogden Lighting
Design, Inc.**
200 Park Avenue South, Suite 1401
New York, NY 10003
T +1 212 674 5580
F +1 212 254 2712
info@hlblighting.com
www.hlblighting.com
The Cooper Union

Parsons Brinckerhoff HQ
One Penn Plaza
New York, NY 10119
T +1 212 465 5000
www.pbworld.com
**Ion Orchard; Mizu Hairdressing
Salon**

**Renzo Piano Building Workshop
(RPBW)**
827 Washington Street
New York, NY 10014
T +1 212 400 2302
F +1 212 400 2307
www.rpbw.com
**The Modern Wing, Art Institute
of Chicago**

Vinci Hamp Architects
1147 West Ohio Street
6th Floor
Chicago, Illinois 60642
T +1 312 733 7744
F +1 312 733 4276
vha@vinci-hamp.com
www.vinci-hamp.com
**Chagall's America Windows, Art
Institute of Chicago**

MEXICO

Lux Populi
Plaza San Jacinto 8 int F
San Angel, CP 01000
Mexico D.F.
F +52 55 5025 9105
info@luxpopuli.com
www.luxpopuli.com
**Chagall's America Windows, Art
Institute of Chicago**

ABOUT THE CD

The attached CD can be read on both Windows and Macintosh computers. All the material on the CD is copyright protected and is for private use only.

The CD includes files for all of the plans, sections and elevation drawings included in the book, where available. The drawings for each building are contained in a folder labelled with the project name. They are supplied in two versions: the files with the suffix '.eps' are 'vector' Illustrator EPS files but can be opened using other graphics programs such as Photoshop; all the files with the suffix '.dwg' are generic CAD format files and can be opened in a variety of CAD programs.

Each image file is numbered according to its original location within the book and within a project, reading from left to right and top to bottom of the page, followed by the scale. Hence, '01_01_200.eps' would be the eps version of the first drawing of the first project in the book and has a scale of 1:200.

The generic '.dwg' file format does not support 'solid fill' utilized by many architectural CAD programs. All the information is embedded within the file and can be reinstated within supporting CAD programs. Select the polygon required and change the 'Attributes' to 'Solid', and the colour information should be automatically retrieved. To reinstate the 'Walls'; select all objects within the 'Walls' layer/class and amend their 'Attributes' to 'Solid'.

CREDITS

Images are supplied courtesy of the architects/lighting designers. In all cases every effort has been made to credit the copyright holders, but should there be any omissions or errors the publisher will be pleased to insert the appropriate acknowledgment in any subsequent editions of the book.

133 HOUNDSDITCH, LONDON
Lighting: Maurice Brill Lighting Design; Architect/interior design: Swanke Hayden Connell Architects; Photographs courtesy MBLD

ACROPOLIS MUSEUM, PARTHENON GALLERY
Client: OCNAM (Dr Pandermalis); Lighting (daylight and electric): Arup (Florence Lam, Vasiliki Malakasi, Katie Davies, Matt Franks, Tim Hanson); Architects: Bernard Tschumi Architects, Photiadis Architects, Costis Skroumbelos Associates; Main contractor: Aktor; Photographs courtesy Arup

ANDAZ HOTEL, THE STUDIO
Lighting: Neil Knowles, Elektra Lighting; Interior: Stuart Wilsdon, Wilsdon Design Associates; Project Manager: Confluence; Electrical Contractor: CES; Equipment: PJR Engineering, LightGraphix, Precision Lighting, iLight

ARMANI GINZA TOWER
Lighting: Speirs + Major; Photography: Ramon Pratt (p150 & p153 top right), other images courtesy Speirs + Major

BRIDGE PAVILION, ZARAGOZA
Lighting: Bartenback LichtLabor; Architect: Zaha Hadid Architects; Photography: Fernando Guerra

CHAGALL'S AMERICA WINDOWS, ART INSTITUTE OF CHICAGO
Client: The Art Institute of Chicago Lighting: Thomas Paterson, Lux Populi; Architect: Vinci Hamp Architects (Daniel Roush, John Vinci, Philip Hamp); Design and construction: Bernice Chu, Sara Urizar; Photography: Eric Hausman

CHAN RESTAURANT
Owner: Chandris Hotels; Lighting: L+DG Thomas Gravanis Lighting Architects; Architect: Andy Martin Associates; Photographer: Paterakis Studio, Chagall ®/ © ADAGP, Paris and DACS, London 2011

CHARLES DE GAULLE AIRPORT SATELLITE 4
Lighting: Light Cibles; Architect: ADP; Perspectives: ADPI; Images courtesy Light Cibles

CHESAPEAKE ENERGY CORPORATION CAR PARK
Lighting designer/architect: Elliot and Associates; Photography: Scott McDonald © Hedrich Blessing

CNIT, PARIS
Lighting: Light Cibles; Architect: BCA; Photography: Fabrice Rambert

COOPER UNION FOR THE ADVANCEMENT OF SCIENCE AND ART
Client: The Cooper Union for the Advancement of Science and Art; Lighting: Horton Lees Brogden Lighting Design; Design architect/ architect of record: Morphosis; Associate architect: Gruzen Samton General contractor: FJ Sciame Construction Co; Electrical engineer/MEP consultant: IBE; Consulting Engineers, Syska Hennessy; Background drawings: Morphosis/Gruzen Samton with overlay notations by HLBLD; Photographs courtesy HLBLD

CRYSTALS OF CITYCENTER, LAS VEGAS
Lighting: Focus Lighting (Principal designer Paul Gregory; Lighting designers Juan Pablo Lira, Stephanie Daigle, Michael Cummins, Hilary Manners); Architect: Studio Daniel Libeskind; Interior architect: Rockwell Group; Architect of record: Adamson Associates; Photographs courtesy Focus Lighting

DELOITE HQ
Lighting installation: Studio Steven Scott; Programming assistance: Morten Krath, Pragmasoft; Architect: Vossloh Schwabe LEDLine; Control: e:cue MediaEngine; Photographs courtesy Steven Scott

EnBW HQ
Client: EnBW Systems Infrastructure Support; User: EnBW energy Baden-Wuerttemberg Corp; Lighting: Licht Kunst Licht; Architect: RKW Rhode Kellermann Wawrowsky Achitektur+Städtebau; Photography: Lukas Roth

ESPA AT THE EUROPE HOTEL
Client: ESPA at The Europe Hotel & Resort; Spa operator: ESPA International; Lighting: DPA Lighting Consultants (Nick Hoggett, Partner; Richard Bolt, Associate); Interior design: HBA/Hirsch Bedner Associates; Photographs courtesy DPA

GSC GROUP OFFICES
Lighting: Cline Bettridge Bernstein;

Lighting supplier: Traxon; Architect: Skidmore, Owings & Merrill LLP (New York office); Photography: Jimmy Cohrssen

ION ORCHARD
Lighting: Lighting Planners Associates Inc. and Parsons Brinckerhoff Pte, Singapore; Architect: Benoy Architects; Photography: Lighting Planners Associates Inc. (pages 160 & 165), Orchard Turn Development Pte. Ltd. (page 163); Product drawings: Krislite

ITSU SUSHI, HEATHROW
Lighting: Cinimod Studio; Photography: Cinimod Studio

PRIVATE RESIDENCE
Lighting: Derek Porter Studio; Architect: Hufft Projects Photography: Michael Spillers © mspillers 2011

JOYERÍA D JEWELLERY OUTLET
Lighting: Architectural Lighting Solutions (Anton Amann, Mikel Juarrero); Photographs courtesy Architectural Lighting Solutions

KPMG OFFICES
Client: KPMG; Lighting: Light Bureau; Architect: Swanke Hayden Connell; Electrical engineer: Aecom Electrical contractor: Phoenix Electrical; Photography: Nick Hufton, Hufton and Crow

LIGHTCATCHER, WHATCOM MUSEUM
Lighting: Candela; Architect: Olson Kundig Architects; Photography: Tim Bies (page 83); Ben Benschneider (pages 84 & 85)

MANDARIN ORIENTAL HOTEL
Lighting: Isometrix Lighting Design; Interior design: Studio Urquiola; Images © Mandarin Oriental, Barc.

MET HOTEL
Client: Chandris Hotels; Lighting: L+DG Thomas Gravanis Lighting Architects; Architect: ZEGE SA; M&E consultant: JEPA Ltd; Photographer: Paterakis Studio

MIZU HAIRDRESSING SALON
Lighting: Parsons Brinckerhoff (Jeffrey Berg, Christopher Leone, John Powell); Architect of record: CBT Architects (Karl Brown, John Cretecos, Ron Awenson, Alfred Wojciechowski); Design architect: Niall McLaughlin Architects (Maria Fulford, Niall McLaughlin); MEP engineer: Richard D Kimball Company Inc. (Keith Giguere); Photographs courtesy Parsons Brinckerhoff

THE MODERN WING, ART INSTITUTE OF CHICAGO
Lighting: Arup; Design architect: Renzo Piano Building Workshop; Executive architect: Interactive Design; Structure and services engineer: Arup; Drawings: Renzo Piano Building Workshop Photography: Charles G Young; Interactive Design: Arup

MURALE BEAUTY RETAIL OUTLET
Lighting and interior design: Burdifilek, Photographs courtesy Diego Burdi, Burdifilek

NATIONAL CONVENTION CENTRE, QATAR
Lighting: Light + Design Associates; Concept architect: Arata Isozaki and i-Net; Executive architect: Halcrow; Architect: RHWL; Design development, manufacture and installation: JT Kalmar; Photographs courtesy Light + Design Associates

OPPOSITE HOUSE HOTEL
Lighting: Isometrix Lighting + Design; Architect: Kengo Kuma Architects; Images © Opposite House, Beijing

PALACE OF INTERNATIONAL FORUMS
Lighting: Pfarré Lighting Design, Munich; Interior architect: Ippolito Fleitz Group; LED rings manufacturer: Korona Leuchten; Wall fitting manufacturer: Lichtlauf; Photography: Andreas Focke

PARLIAMENT ASSEMBLY HALL, LIECHTENSTEIN
Client: Federal State Parliament, Vaduz; Lighting: Licht Kunst Licht; Architect: Hansjörg Göritz Architecture, Hannover; Frick Architektur, Liechtenstein; Photography: Lukas Roth

PLATFORM FIVE, SUNDERLAND STATION
Client: Nexus; Lighting: Jason Bruges Studio (Creative Director Jason Bruges, Project Lead Jonathon Hodges); Computational design: Karsten Schmidt, PostSpectacular; Architect: David Benison, Sadler Brown Architecture; Project engineer: Richard Eakin, Arup; Electrical and mechanical installation: Peter Read, LX Engineering; Art consultant: Andrew Knight; Photographs courtesy Jason Bruges Studio

RESIDENTIAL SPA
Lighting: Lighting Design International; Architect: Carmody Groarke; Photography © Christian Richter

ROPEMAKER PLACE, LONDON
Client: British Land; Ceiling lighting design: Arup Associates, Zumtobel Lighting, SAS International, Stortfort Interiors; Architect/ consulting engineer: Arup Associates

THE ROTUNDA, BIRMINGHAM
Client: Urban Splash; Lighting: Mindseye Lighting; Lighting tubes and control system: Projected Image Digital; Architect: Glen Howells Architects; Photographs courtesy Mindseye Lighting

RUENTEX TUNHUA-RENAI CONDOMINIUM LOBBY
Client: Ruentex Development Co Ltd; Lighting: CMA Lighting Design; Architect: Wong and Wong Associates; Interior design: Holly Design; Photography: Jeffery Chen, Precious Stone Studio

SEGERSTROM CONCERT HALL
Lighting: Cline Bettridge Bernstein Lighting Design; Architects: Pelli Clarke Pelli Architects; Gruen Architects; Custom chandelier fixture manufacture by Designplan Lighting Inc (USA); Photography: RMA Photography Inc, Douglas Salin

SHEIKH ZAYED BIN SULTAN AL NAHYAN MOSQUE
Lighting: Speirs + Major; Photography: Lars Kirsten Anderson (page 90), all other images courtesy Speirs + Major

SNOG FROZEN YOGHURT
Architecture and lighting: Cinimod Studio; Branding and graphics: ICO Design; Main contractor: Allan Nuttall; Architectural lighting: Philips Lighting; Ceiling control system: amBX; Signage and light boxes: the Lettering Centre; Photography: Cinimod Studio

SOUND NIGHTCLUB, PHUKET
Lighting: Inverse Lighting Design Interior design: Orbit Design Bangkok in association with Bed Supperclub; Photography: Basil Childers and Bernhard Bstieler

ZA-KOENJI PERFORMING ARTS THEATRE
Lighting: LIGHTDESIGN INC Architect: Toyo Ito and Associates Architects; Photography © Toshio Kaneko

192